THE POWER OF 10

THE POWER OF 10

*A practice for engaging your voice of wisdom
to be the greatest you—the you who is meant to be.*

TJIKKO PUBLISHING
2501 N. Harwood Street, Suite 2001
Dallas, Texas 75201
tjikko.com

ISBN: 978-0-9909753-1-1
LCCN: 2015908276

Wisdom tells me I'm nothing. Love tells me I'm everything. Between the two flows the river of my life. —Nisargadatta Maharaj

CONTENTS

PREFACE

This work began as a bequest. For most of my life, I feared the ocean, sharks, and loss of control. This all changed. In the course of a year, my marriage imploded, I gave up an established career to start over, and my mother was diagnosed with a cancer that would take her life. With sorrow, uncertainty, and the inevitability of loss weighing heavily on me, I realized my deepest fears were not somewhere out in the dark water but much closer.

I had spent years in motion focused on building and achieving—acquiring one more thing or climbing to the next level. But why? Maybe I would have said, "Independence." That wasn't really true though. I was already free; at any moment I could choose whatever way of being I desired. What I didn't want to admit was that I depended on others for acceptance, even affirmation. Stripped of the cloak of identity—no longer husband, partner, son—who would I be? The tokens of achievement and many possessions accumulated along the way seemed meaningless and my heart felt hollow.

Within the flux of change, a sobering awareness emerged: I had been living so profoundly out of alignment with what mattered, not only hadn't I been my best self for them, I hadn't even been *me*. Recognizing the need to break the patterns of the past, I decided to illuminate what long-held fears I was able to articulate. Maybe shedding light on their roots would help me understand the feelings emerging in the present.

Not long after committing to this course, I volunteered to crew on a small boat crossing the Pacific Ocean. Together, the captain, his wife, one other crewmember, and I planned to sail more than 2,500 nautical miles in the latitudes of the coldest waters and beyond the range of any practical rescue. During our many weeks at sea, we would be tested by the boat, the ocean, and the weather. The risks, both foreseeable and unforeseeable, prompted me to evaluate my legacy—should I not return, what of any value could I pass along?

Mere possessions, so quickly dispersed, would offer little recompense in exchange for the love so many had shared. After decades of living, surely there was something more I could offer. What words might I pen on the available bit of paper, seal tightly in a bottle, and throw overboard in the hope of transmitting a message of gratitude to those on a distant shore?

I began to write. Through writing, I began to explore, and through exploring, to discover. First purpose, then a practice.

My purpose—indeed our purpose—is to express love. Some might dismiss this, saying, "What a lofty ideal" or "How sweet . . . " or even ridicule the notion. But love, as the theologian Paul Tillich pointed out, is the foundation of all power.[1] It provides the will to transcend in the presence of resistance. More important, love *is* what matters. If you doubt this, take a moment and imagine a world governed by love. What better way of life could there be?

Within this greater purpose, my role is to champion the voice of wisdom, the voice that tells you whether you are conducting or impeding love. Maybe you experience love in relationship to god, family, work, or nature. And as you consciously engage your voice of wisdom, you learn to channel the love you sense in *one* area of life into *all* areas of life—your *whole* life. Living this way restores the deep abiding happiness that flows from being your best self and living in harmony with your purpose.

With respect to what follows, I make no claim to any original ideas or that this practice will serve any other person. My aim in publishing this work is to memorialize my intentions for living: to live meaningfully and lovingly while positively influencing those I touch. Thus, what began as a testament became a declaration for being. In this regard, I have only now begun to live.

ABOUT THE NUMBER 10

Why ten? Why not three or nine or twenty-seven?

The number itself is an even, natural number, the base of the most common numbering system in spoken or written language, presumably adapted from our inherited biology of having ten digits.

In numerical form, it is written using "1" and "0," numbers that represent the two states of a binary system, much like the poles of human existence: everything and nothing, consciousness and unconsciousness, masculine and feminine, yin and yang, the earthly and the divine. Given any two such opposing forces, a natural tension develops between them. The question is: How can we exploit this tension for our benefit?

In what follows, ten represents the sum of five questions and five guiding principles; one represents advocacy (I am everything), and zero represents inquiry (I am nothing). And more: the numbers one and zero point toward the tension between these two contradictory but related positions or forces. (*Wisdom tells me I'm nothing. Love tells me I'm everything.*) This tension provides the energy to propel us toward wholeness and, in turn, happiness.

ABOUT THE NAMES OF PEOPLE IN THIS BOOK

Every person mentioned in this work is real. The names, except for those of well-known historical personages, are not, but are derived from two principal sources: the photographers and explorers of the twentieth century.

Many of the famous of that era—from Gandhi to Churchill to Martin Luther King Jr.—were unequivocally "great" men and women who shaped the course of history for future generations and whose examples continue to uplift and inspire us. The power of their achievements resides in how they help us imagine something infinitely greater than the status quo, worth pursuing regardless of personal risk or benefit.

Photojournalists and explorers can be similarly inspirational. Armed with nothing more than a rangefinder and a roll of film, photojournalists set out to document the edges of our world in faithful detail. Few forms of media captured our attention and provoked us more than documentary photographs, disparate images of everything from everyday urban life to the horrors of war. Confronted by the truth, we could no longer say, "I didn't know." And while photographers expanded our awareness of what is, explorers challenged our perspective of what could be. Witnessing Jacques Cousteau plumb the depths of the seas and the astronauts of the Apollo missions venture into the vast reaches of space, we were inspired to believe that no boundary could limit our dreams.

From such men and women we learned never to say, "I can't believe."

Though some of these extraordinary people are not well remembered today, they all helped us understand both *what is* in our lives and *what is possible*. This quality of personal transcendence links all those who appear on these pages. Their extraordinary courage and fortitude spark our imaginations and, in the words of André Gide, help us understand that "to discover new oceans we must be willing to lose sight of the shore."

INTRODUCTION

If you set out to be less than you are capable of being, I warn you, you will be deeply unhappy for the rest of your life. —Abraham Maslow

What do you most desire? for yourself? for those you care about? now and for the future? Ask anyone this question, and chances are they will say it is to be happy. Initially, some people may respond with a more specific desire: to win the lottery, have a family, travel every continent, or even to make a difference in the world.

But then ask them why. *Why* do you want to win the lottery? *Why* do you want to travel the world? Keep asking why, and follow the thread until there is only one remaining response. At the end of all the whys, the answer will almost always be *to be happy*—or sometimes *to be healthy and happy*. Not only do we want to be happy, we want those we love to be happy too or, more expansively, *healthy* and happy.

But what do these words really mean?

The dictionary says the word "health" is derived from "wholeness," a state of complete physical, social, and mental wellbeing—healthy body, heart, and mind. "Happiness," on the other hand, refers to a state of joy, compassion, and love balanced by equanimity. Health, meaning wholeness, in concert with abiding happiness, improves the quality of our lives and perhaps even the quantity of our days.

Notice how we think of each as a state of being. We don't want to "do happy" or "have happy." We say we want to *be* happy, we want to *be* healthy, and we want our loved ones to *be* happy and healthy as well. Ultimately, whether we realize it or not, we are all seeking happiness in our daily lives.

But for most people, happiness is a mysteriously elusive condition. Few of us know how to deliberately attain a state of happiness or how to maintain it when we encounter it by chance. Too often we relate happiness to *having* something— an expensive home, new car, or position of authority. Yet we discover that people who live in expensive houses or have nice cars or hold important positions aren't necessarily any happier than anyone else.

We might, on the other hand, think of happiness as *doing* something—taking a vacation to Hawaii or eating a box of chocolate chip cookies. But Hawaii is far away, and it turns out that even in Hawaii, people can be unhappy. And eating a box of cookies? Of course it's wonderful in the moment, but once we've eaten a certain number, the pleasure is gone.

Happiness, then, is not in the having or doing that people grow accustomed to; people who are happy don't have to buy anything or go anywhere. Happiness is in their being. That's all there is to it: the secret to happiness is to *be* happy. The good news is that you don't have to buy an expensive house, spend years climbing a corporate ladder, or travel to a faraway place to be happy. In fact, there is no waiting time at all. Happiness is here and available right now—and it's free.

Sounds easy enough. So why aren't we spending more time being happy?

The reality is that even though we all know this in the core of our being, most of us still don't understand how to sustain happiness.

The Pursuit of Happiness

As you seek more happiness in your life, you soon realize that *pursuing* happiness will not *produce* happiness. As a goal in itself, happiness is almost impossible to achieve, because no single set of actions or activities will call it into being. Merely thinking happy thoughts or saying nice things or acting in positive ways will not transport you to a state of happiness. Nor is happiness available for purchase. Buying something you covet may create momentary happiness, but the thrill is short-lived. True happiness requires a more holistic approach.

Happiness is derived from *living into* our greatest potential in all areas of our lives. By "living into," we mean the moment-to-moment practice of aligning our bodies, hearts, and minds with the positive expression of our intentions until we manifest our purpose through our thoughts, words, and actions. In other words, it is about consciously choosing to be our best selves until it becomes an unconscious way of being. Through living into the greatest potential in each domain of our lives, we learn to realize wholeness and, through wholeness, happiness. By their nature, *wholeness* and *happiness* are inextricably intertwined.

Although one might be tempted to associate a devotion to happiness with some inherently selfish pursuit, it is equally selfless. Happiness gives rise to generosity and compassion; happy people want others to be happy too. Moreover, happiness simply can't persist in the midst of suffering. (How can you be completely happy when there is disharmony in any part of your life?)

Sustained happiness presupposes wholeness, and wholeness depends partly on the wellbeing of the other people in our lives—a virtuous cycle. Indeed, because happy people have transformed their narrowly selfish concerns, their strongest motivations are often altruistic. It follows that happier people are better suited to effect positive change in the world. Thinking, speaking, and acting in a wholesome way, we learn how to elevate others. We may have no real method of measuring our influence, but one thing is certain: the world is hungry for beauty, truth, and goodness. Bringing our whole selves into being, we nourish the lives of others.

In contrast, when we choose not to live up to our potential, we feel a gnawing dissatisfaction that results from living an unhealthy, incomplete way of life. Many of us live our entire lives with this discontent, ignoring the feeling or drowning it in work, alcohol, shopping, or other distractions that desensitize us to our dissatisfaction. Or, too willingly, we strive toward a contrived tomorrow to mask our fear of living into our full capabilities today.

We might, for example, dream of having an abundance of money and tirelessly pursue the acquisition of wealth. But even if we amass what we once thought was enough, satisfaction will not last, because we will need to work to preserve what we have and still earn more. Reaching each new goal, we find the number representing our happiness receding further into the future. And even if we are temporarily satisfied with our newfound wealth, we worry about losing it, because happiness is then vulnerable to fluctuations in our bank account.

Anytime we rely solely on something outside ourselves for validation or fulfillment, we abdicate our power—maybe even our responsibility—to create our own happiness. We ignore what really matters until some external event jolts us awake. Sometimes it's painful, such as the trauma of death,

The domain of *self* refers to "I" or "me" and, more specifically, the alignment (or misalignment) of one's body, heart, and mind.

The domain of *others* refers to our relationships with the other people in our lives.

The domain of the *future* refers to the future at every stage—the next second, the next hour, the next year, the next generation, and so on.

The domain of the *present* refers to this moment, the very instant you are reading these words—the now that is the culmination of all past moments.

And finally, the domain of *choice* refers to our uniquely human ability to choose thoughts, words, and actions while simultaneously considering how our choices influence the other domains.

While it helps to identify the domains separately, in reality, each is merely a facet of an undivided whole and limited only by the boundaries of our concerns, whether they encompass oneself or another or extend outward to the whole world.

When we reflect on each inquiry, we increase our awareness of *what is*, the current state of our being. For example, the second question, corresponding to the domain of others, is simply, "How do I impact others?" This question helps reveal how our thoughts, words, and actions individually and collectively affect the people whose lives we touch. While *what is* may be perfect in its way, in asking the question, we create the space for learning how it might be even better.

We all wrestle with the questions that follow in some form, so having a structure to engage them will help. For this reason, each inquiry is paired with a corresponding guiding principle that describes our intentions. For example, you may have a vague, unarticulated notion about being a positive influence on others. Your response to the query "How do I impact others?" may take form as the intention, *do unto others as I would have done unto me.* Or you might choose as your guiding principle, "be kind." The right one will emerge when your body, heart, and mind agree it is true. Whatever guiding principle you choose, once you declare your commitment to it, it becomes yours to advocate, even as it evolves or you refine it over time.

The five guiding principles advanced in the Advocacy section inform our responses to the questions. You are welcome to adopt these principles as they are or use them as patterns for creating your own. Whatever words you choose, the purpose of any guiding principle is to prescribe a best practice for achieving wholeness. Wholeness, or the state of being whole, emerges from the practice of being your *greatest self* in all the domains of your life over time. Therefore, as we become more intentional about creating the life we desire, it is important to keep asking, *what would the best me think, say, or do, irrespective of circumstances?* In other words, a long-term commitment to a guiding principle forms the basis of a sacred vow to be the best you possible, transcending any immediate, competing desire—even when lesser impulses arise, such as when others express unkindness toward us.

A Practice for Engaging Your Voice of Wisdom

The Power of 10 is neither a theory nor a belief, but a *practice.* Nor does it require shaving our heads, sewing our own clothes, or quitting our jobs and moving to an ashram. It is an everyday practice for bringing wholeness (and thereby happiness) into our lives and creating a better relation-ship with the environment we live in. Daily life and the people we come into contact with serve as the objects of our practice, as well as our teachers. We grow more in a day of interacting with others around us than in a year of sitting alone high atop a mountain contemplating some desired future.

The intention of this practice is to engage your voice of wisdom. Since first learning to speak, we have been in a con-tinual dialogue with ourselves. (If you doubt this, try to sit quietly for ten minutes without a thought going through your mind. Good luck making it even one minute.) What arises is not limited to just one voice, either. Within us exists a multitude of voices contributing to the conversation—the voices of doubt, certainty, complaint, contentment, judg-ment, admiration, and many other versions of our "selves."

These voices know us better than another human being ever could, at least in terms of how we think. And they con-tinually comment on our choices. The voice of wanting says, *go ahead and eat another chocolate chip cookie*. The voice of responsibility says, *if you eat another cookie, you will upset your stomach and feel miserable*. And then there is the most inces-sant voice, the voice of dissatisfaction, always comparing and judging and saying to you, *things would be better if only . . .*

No one of these voices is you. You are more than any one voice or any one feeling; you are infinitely bigger. While lesser voices make demands and try to dominate the conversation (and our lives), each is a temporary fluc-tuation of the wind. Wind occurs over a range of scales, from an occasional gentle breeze to a hurricane that lasts for days. Like the wind, voices swirl inside us, stirring up emotions. While they may bring with them the cool breeze of equanimity or a hot gust of anger, it is important not to be fooled into thinking these voices *are* all you are. When the voice of anger rages in frustration, it is helpful to remember *you* are not anger; unless you offer it a place to reside, anger is merely a transient experience. With practice, you can learn to stand up to anger like a mighty oak or to bend and let it pass over you like a pliant willow. But if you make the mistake of believing the anger is what you are, you give in to it and allow it to carry you away, a leaf in a gale.

While it is unwise to identify with and act upon these voices, it is also foolish to suppress them or ignore the subtle ways they alter your course. Be alert to changes in the wind; they tell you things you have not yet fully realized or, perhaps, accepted. They can also warn you of an impending storm, something we all seek shelter from in more or less skillful ways. Listening helps: sometimes their rantings are a disguised plea for a stronger voice to confront and control them, to transform them into a functional partner. Your inner critic, for example, is also your inner champion; telling you what you are doing wrong, it encourages you to do things better. Given the continual bantering in our heads, why not listen to the one voice that serves you best, the *voice of wisdom*?

Though all voices are part of you, the voice of wisdom is the integral, positive expression of all the other voices. But unlike the others, the voice of wisdom is both you and something greater than you. It has a vested interest in you, as well as its own aspirations and motives. It exists to ensure health and happiness. And its purpose is made evident through bringing forward the best you in service of something greater than yourself.

While any number of voices appeal to one part of us—the sensual pleasures of the body or the communal nature of the heart or the rational machinations of the mind—only the voice of wisdom satisfies all three. Only when there is accord, without preference or reservation, will you know the voice of wisdom is speaking.

Like the moon, the voice of wisdom rises above the weathered sky. It is your ever-present companion who knows your deepest desires, your best-kept secrets, and your highest capabilities. A companion who knows the many "yous" presented to the different people in your life. Who knows every book you have read, every class you've taken, every piece of advice you have received, and who has shared every sensation and every feeling, and witnessed every insight and epiphany.

Even though you can't always hear it, you know the voice of wisdom is trying to speak to you. You know this. No matter how long you have ignored it, as you summon it through inquiry and advocacy, it begins to make itself known. It speaks in the silent spaces between your thoughts. Hearing it is only a matter of listening.

Learning to Listen to Your Voice of Wisdom

For reasons that may never be clear, most of us change only in response to suffering, often when the painful results of past choices become apparent. Indeed, the mysterious silver lining to the black cloud of suffering is that it illuminates behavior that has given rise to our current condition and motivates personal transformation. Unlike pain, however, a physical or psychological discomfort from which we recoil instinctually, suffering is often no more than fear and lamentation, the fierce resistance with which we *react* to pain. In other words, pain is inevitable; suffering is largely avoidable.

The point is, transformation can occur *without* such misery. Through the practice of engaging the voice of wisdom and making healthy choices in accord with our intentions, we build the capacity to improve our lives directly. And as we learn how to do this effectively, each healthy choice we make boosts our immunity to suffering.

Imagine a time recently when you felt you were not your best self. It's not hard for most of us to find an example of less than exemplary behavior. Now review the incident; visualize your thoughts, words, and actions, and ask your voice of wisdom for advice—if you could go back in time, what would have been helpful? Then listen. What should you have done differently?

Now imagine yourself acting on that advice. Replay the scene in your mind and envision developing the habit of acting more wisely whenever you fall short. Then practice being your best self—learning to fill the gap between impulse and response with gratefulness and grace. And continue until it becomes intuitive. The next time similar circumstances arise, maybe you will remember to consult your voice of wisdom and find something helpful to say or do.

When the winds of your lesser voices threaten to overwhelm you, just remember: you can say *no*. If, for example, the voice of anger continues to howl, step outside. Go for a walk. Take a deep breath. Get some fresh air. The voice of wisdom is always available once you become present to it.

Imagine the moon—or look up to where it is suspended in the fathomless depths of the sky, and remember to be understanding and compassionate when you return to yourself. The winds can no more change the essential nature of your being than blow the moon out of its orbit.

Like any new practice, the Power of 10 may feel awkward and artificial at first. It helps to remember that the questions and guiding principles of the practice are not tasks to master, but companions on your journey through life.

The Power of 10 teaches you to lean forward until the natural "gravity" of wholeness pulls you forward. Lean forward by examining the reality of *what is* by wrestling with the question of inquiry: What do my body, heart, and mind agree to be true in each of the domains of my life?

Living in relationship to these questions and guiding principles enables us to explore them more deeply—allowing the questions to evolve until they become sources of wisdom of their own. But these benefits cannot be fully realized until the practice itself becomes one of our mental attitudes, directing our attention to significant events as they happen in the course of our daily lives. Once we commit to our guiding principles, the attraction of harmonious living draws us toward manifesting the potential of *what can be*. Over time, the practice helps us summon forth our voice of wisdom to identify our purpose, recognize our influence on others, achieve our goals, bring real awareness to the moment, and more consciously direct our power to create.

As we begin to choose our thoughts, words, and actions with greater awareness, we recognize how our choices not only create our identities and experiences, but also co-create the environment we live in. With this realization comes the responsibility to create the conditions of deep, abiding happiness for ourselves and for those who surround us.

Our Toolkit

How do we remember these questions? And how do we manage to *re-mind* ourselves of them? Perhaps the most basic mnemonic, one that is always with us, is the first tool of exploration: our hands. Our nondominant hand is our *hand of inquiry*, reminding us of our questions. Each finger, beginning with our index finger, corresponds to an inquiry:

- Who am I?
- How do I impact others?
- How will I spend this day?
- What is happening in this moment?
- How do we become our greatest selves?

Our dominant hand serves as the *hand of advocacy*, reminding us of our guiding principles. Again starting with the index finger, each finger corresponds to a principle:

- Stand Tall
- Be Kind
- Plan Ahead
- Let Go
- Choose Love

Our hands remind us of the best that is possible within us and the principles we must uphold to make this possibility a reality. Wherever we go, they remind us of the distilled wisdom they symbolize. Our hands reinforce our power to create by linking each question to choices that either create wholeness or move us further away from it. By inviting wholeness into our lives, we fulfill ourselves and create the basis for sustained happiness even as we continue to reveal the potential of *what can be* in the world around us.

Let us begin.

PART 1: INQUIRY

Learn from yesterday, live for today, hope for tomorrow. The important thing is not to stop questioning. —Albert Einstein

We are curious beings. It is our nature to explore. As children, we began exploring using our hands. We reached out and grasped objects, pulled them to us, shook them, smelled them, and, more often than not, put them in our mouths and tasted them. Though we didn't know the words, we began to make meaning: the fruit tastes good; the peel tastes not so good. We laughed a lot, cried sometimes, but always continued to explore.

Over time the gift of language allowed us to examine the world by asking questions. In fact, we asked lots of questions. Some to discern facts:

What's this? What's that?
When will we get there?
What's for dinner?
And some that were more philosophical in nature:
Where did we come from?
Why are we here?
Where do we go when we die?

But as adults, most of our questions concern our relationships with the environment we live in and the people within it:

What is your name? Where are you from?

If you could go anywhere in the world, where would you go?

Which do you like better, apple juice or orange juice?

We catalogue answers to these questions in our memory for future reference: Barry, from Boston. Hawaii. Orange juice. In storing these answers in our minds, we attach qualitative judgments based on our feelings or experiences: Barry seems like a nice guy. I've seen pictures of Hawaii, and it looks like paradise. Apple juice is too sweet; freshly squeezed orange juice is the best.

Later, encountering similar circumstances, we access our memories of experiences to help us evaluate the present. For example, the first time you drank the juice of an orange, someone told you it was "orange juice." The name "orange juice" became a frame around which you draped a memory of the experience. Now, the words and experience are indistinguishable; the act of naming a thing limits the variability of interpretation. As Tennyson cautioned, "Words, like nature, half reveal and half conceal the soul within."

When asked to describe what it is like to squeeze oranges and drink a glass of orange juice, you can probably envision an experience or a compilation of them. Pressed to provide details, you might begin by picturing the fruit, with its pebble-grained texture, its weight in your hand, and the way it smells, especially if you scratch its rind or break it open with your fingers. Perhaps you can imagine the weight of the full glass in your hand as you draw it to you and that first smell before you taste it, the fragrance of tart citrus. You might even describe the taste in your mouth as it first touches your tongue: sweetness followed by the acidic tang with the bits of fruit. By now your mouth may even be watering though you haven't had a drink.

But why? Why would your mouth water just because you're thinking the words *orange juice*?

Before asking what the juice in the glass tastes like, you may already have an answer in mind.

Once we have tasted orange juice, it is impossible to un-taste it and difficult to fully experience it again. The next time we pick up a glass, the always already knowing voice of experience tells us what to expect. Our memories indelibly color our perception of what *actually is*, the glass of juice presently in our hand. In effect, we may have already decided what the experience will be before it even happens—*this will be too sweet, because it's "apple juice," and I prefer "orange juice."*

By its nature, the act of deciding kills any other possibilities. After all, the Latin root *cide* means "to kill." The moment you decide what the experience is going to be, you relinquish the opportunity to taste anew.

While such instant, unconscious interpretation of raw sensation helps us in many respects, the same reflexive perceptions that spare us having to focus on every task, however mundane, also distort our connection to direct experience. Ever vigilant to protect us from harm, our internal voices intervene. Drawing upon the catalogue of our experiences and the words we associate with them, we substitute memories for fresh experience.

As human beings, we have a natural desire for consistency. We instinctively give free rein to our voice of experience to form snap judgments and instant opinions. While this process is efficient and often results in the "correct" answer, it also precludes authentic experience. Moreover, even if we can ignore an automatic response and *sense* something as it is at a particular moment, we may feel disoriented if this sensory impression conflicts with our expectations, especially of routines and relationships we most take for granted. Unexpected revelations sometimes provoke a deep internal dissonance. But this very unease can spur an important internal dialogue or debate. If we enter this debate with an open mind, we might make discoveries that expand our awareness, sharpen our perceptions, and multiply the possibilities we see before us.

We hinder our growth or impede it altogether when we become too certain—when we "know," when we stop questioning, and, especially, when our minds are closed to new possibilities. Certainty is a brittle delusion that renders us increasingly fragile in a world of continual change. Believing the past predicts the future or dismissing something new leaves us unable to see that what we *assume* is progress may instead be an undetected current carrying us far away. And one day we may find ourselves crashing on a shore we didn't know existed and wonder, *how did I get here? What was I thinking? I thought I was on a course for happiness, but this is a dramatically different place.*

So how can we reawaken our ability to experience things anew and expand our perspective without becoming disoriented and anxious? How can we remember to savor the juice each time anew or learn to hear what someone is trying to tell us, even when they don't know the right words?

We can engage in *inquiry*.

Inquiry is a practice of living in relation to questions of meaning, both qualitative and quantitative. Such questions inevitably shift our focus from knowing to wondering, tapping into our natural inclination to learn and create. They heighten our connection with reality while simultaneously increasing our understanding of one or more domains of our life. Critical to the success of this endeavor is to ask open-ended questions, free of judgment, while remaining receptive and unattached to the responses. Asking open-ended questions, we are forced to reexamine not only the object of our attention, but the subject—the part of us asking the question. What is the nature and origin of the question? Persisting in these inquiries, we amass a personal body of knowledge, and in the process acquire a deeper understanding of our own interests and perceptions.

Restate almost any declaration as a question, and you begin to examine what you only assumed to be true. Instead of thinking, *I prefer orange juice to apple juice,* consider asking, *which juice do I prefer?* A simple how, what, when, where or why widens the field of possibilities. You might prefer apple to orange juice if the apple juice is fresh-pressed rather than reconstituted concentrate. Now consider expanding the field further, perhaps asking, *what is my favorite juice?* A thoughtful response to this expanded inquiry might entail sampling a wide variety of juices, ending with the surprising discovery that your overall favorite is pomegranate juice. But even if you consider all available options and still choose orange juice, your experience in comparison tasting the other juices with an open mind will probably have increased your interest in tasting it again, and this time with an educated palate.

The more we examine, the greater the number of perspectives we can hold—a broader range of choices, increasing our opportunity to retain the freshness and immediacy of current experience. Similarly, with the right questions, we can better examine our current lives and use the findings to advocate for *what might be*. Because we are naturally inquisitive and continually in dialogue with ourselves, why not reflect on those questions that reverberate in our minds instead of letting the questions choose us? Is it not worth cultivating questions that have the power to transform our lives?

While others may serve particular individuals better, let us begin by examining our five questions of inquiry. Each question is meant to summon our voice of wisdom, engage it in dialogue, and sharpen our perspective on one of the major domains of our life. Whether or not you experience an "aha" moment on first examining them, they are intended to serve as touchpoints for periodic reflection. What's more, our responses to these inquiries take on new meaning over the arc of our lives as our concerns change from, for example, success to significance. However our answers may change, each question serves as an anchor point and source of inspiration, while each guiding principle is a call to action in each of the five domains.

To give the questions more relevance, examine each one as it pertains to three perspectives—*for my self, for others*, and *for living into*—that correspond directly or indirectly to our bodies, hearts, and minds.

- The body (self) is the gateway to our individual experience.
- Our hearts (others) connect us to the other people in our lives.
- Our minds (living into) direct our intentions and will.

Together, these three perspectives provide a more complete rendering of our experience. Similarly, the five inquiries enlarge our current, limited field of view until it becomes an open field of potential. In the clearing, we see what is possible: to live into our greatest potential and in turn, to experience the true happiness that accompanies the satisfaction of being *whole*.

As we begin our journey, it is helpful to remember what we stand to gain from it. The purpose of conducting inquiry is to develop a set of guiding principles, the moral logic and philosophy by which your voice of wisdom navigates. As we evolve or the environment changes, so too will the course of our lives. In response, the voice of wisdom instinctively corrects course, realigning us to our highest potential. If, moment by moment, we personify our best self, and do so in furtherance of something greater, how can we fail to be truly happy?

CHAPTER 1. WHO AM I?

Knowing yourself is the beginning of all wisdom. —Aristotle

Who am I? Ten thousand questions return to this one. Every language, every culture, every spiritual tradition petitions us to answer the question: *Who am I?* The great philosophers of ancient Greece engraved this question on the entrances to their temples. And it has echoed throughout history, from Shakespeare, who advises in *Hamlet* "to thine own self be true," to our contemporary popular culture. In the film *The Matrix*, when Neo meets the Oracle for the first time, the sign above her kitchen door reads: "Know thyself."

This first question invites us to examine the domain of self. With three simple words, the question elicits an almost infinite number of responses. Why? Because we each think, speak, and act in our own unique ways.

We all recognize our obvious physical differences: we are blue-eyed or brown-eyed, tall or short, left-handed or right-handed. Each of us experiences life from a unique vantage point, one based on our unique preferences and experiences. Our *preferences* are an innate disposition toward a certain condition, character, or effect—or, more simply, what we think of as our likes and dislikes.

Even when we agree on the names and circumstances of certain people, places, and things, we still attach different meanings to them. For example, she may remember the big tree in the back yard as the secret hideout where we built a fort, but he may remember it as the high place he fell from and broke his arm. He may remember Aunt Helen as a stern old woman with hands made for spanking, but she thinks of her as the family historian who baked delicious pies. Even identical twins growing up together make meaning in uniquely different ways. Though they may look alike and share the same history, each has a distinctly individual identity and way of relating to the world.

So if we are each unique, does it not follow that each of us has a unique purpose as well? That there is something distinctly ours—some talent, some skill—that offers us the opportunity to manifest our greatest potential? We may even experience an innate calling in the areas where we feel most alive, even if focusing on the term "purpose" can feel intimidating.

Identifying one's "purpose" suggests a lofty goal, like saying, "I will make a billion dollars," or "I will cure cancer," or "I will win an Academy Award." It might even be so, but need it be so grand? Maybe it is far simpler. Perhaps the secret to identifying your purpose is not in describing some aspirational future state. Rather, it is about connecting to what you are already great at, transforming the intuitive into the intentional by bringing forth that talent for your own and others' benefit—manifesting the you that is already meant to be.

If you live for creating businesses, your purpose is about building organizations to solve problems that matter. If you are brilliant at research, then it is about spending time solving rational problems. If you are a natural performer and want to enrich the lives of others, then it is about spending more time entertaining. What could be a better purpose than

- to catalyze entrepreneurship?
- to extend human life?
- to make people laugh?

It makes sense, does it not, that your true purpose has less to do with achievements, whatever their magnitude, than in being the best, most authentic you? Being the best you may have a scope as large as the entire world or as small as a single person you love with all your heart. However you express it, you know when your purpose is shining through by the way you feel. Experience tells us this—what happens when you're being the real, best you? You feel alive. Happy.

The challenge for us all is the same: to choose to manifest what we are truly great at in this moment and in each moment in the future. What we choose to be, we become. To be our authentic, best selves, each of us must choose to be that self now, in the next moment, in the following moment, and so on. As we choose, we create the experience of the present and lay the foundation for the future.

A reasonable person might ask, "How does finding your purpose really make a difference in your life?" Or somewhat more bluntly, "What's the 'cash value' of connecting with your purpose?"

Consider a few examples of people who have clearly found a response to the question: *Who am I?* Although these people are well known for their accomplishments and for living unapologetically on their own terms, their greatness arose from consciously *living into* their purpose—simply by aligning their thoughts, words, and actions with their true nature.

Picasso, one of the twentieth century's most influential artists, described his purpose this way: "I am always doing

that which I cannot do, in order that I may learn how to do it."
Mother Teresa, a saint in her own lifetime, described herself
as ". . . a little pencil in God's hands."[3] Finally, Muhammad
Ali, whose courage extended beyond the world of sports, put
it this way: "I know where I'm going and I know the truth,
and I don't have to be what you want me to be. I'm free to
be what I want."

In answering this first question, each of these people
declared themselves into being and found the purpose
and meaning to live rich, full lives. Here it is important
to distinguish between being good at something and living your purpose. Although you may be good at many
things, you have only one real purpose in life, though it
may express itself in many different forms. Until you acknowledge that purpose, life can appear slightly distorted,
like a cubist painting: all the angles are visible, but the
essence of your being is out of focus. We see this in others
and, less frequently, in ourselves.

An example to help illustrate the point is the story of a
once-promising prospect in professional baseball. He began
his journey into the big leagues in 1994, working his way up
from double-A to triple-A teams. The major leagues were
only one step away. Then, on the eve of signing with a professional team, he suddenly quit baseball, never to play the
game again. Why? Because he realized that baseball wasn't
his true purpose. The expression of his fullest potential was
outside baseball. But even though he never played baseball
at the highest level, you still might remember him: his name
is Michael Jordan, arguably the best basketball player to ever
set foot on the court.

Despite extraordinary success in basketball, Jordan quit to follow his father's dream that he play baseball—only to realize *his* true passion was basketball. A year after returning to the game, Jordan led the Chicago Bulls to win the first of three straight national championships. In the process, he broke almost every record in the game: five-time league Most Valuable Player, ten-time scoring champion, three-time steals champion, over 32,000 points, 6,000 rebounds, and 5,000 assists. He then went on to write a book about it—*For the Love of the Game*. Michael Jordan loved to play basketball.

Although he was good at almost every sport, his purpose was to elevate the game of basketball. While we might remember him best for his talent on the court, the expression of his purpose took form in different ways over time, from collegiate athlete to professional player to Olympian to team owner. Moreover, by living into his purpose, he inspired many others, both on and off the court. As every kid who laces up a pair of basketball shoes today knows, Michael Jordan found his purpose.

Now ask yourself—what would the world be like if Picasso, Mother Teresa, Muhammad Ali, or even Michael Jordan had not found their purpose?

For My Self

Mediocrity is self-inflicted. Genius is self-bestowed. —*Walter Russell*

Some people know early on exactly what they want to be in life. Think of the kid you knew in grade school who just knew he would grow up to be a firefighter. Let's call him Adam. Decades after graduation, when you bump into him again and ask the inevitable question of what he has done with himself, you learn that Adam has, indeed, gone on to become a firefighter; then he specialized and is now a paramedic. When you ask him what it's like to work as a paramedic, he might describe the numerous false alarms, the mind-numbing paperwork, the financial challenges of municipal budgets, and so on.

But when you ask him why he puts up with it, it's like flipping a switch. Adam's eyes light up and he declares, "Because I get to help people!" Then he describes how everyone has a moment when they have a real emergency, when their life depends on the immediate care of someone who can help them in a way they desperately need. Watching him speak, you have no doubt he enjoys being that person and is quietly proud of making a difference. You can see in his eyes and hear in his tone that he loves being a paramedic and that *Adam's purpose* is to help people in physical distress. Perhaps you even feel calmer in his presence knowing people like him exist.

Like Adam, most of us start with a dream. Maybe you have inherited certain aptitudes from your parents or are attracted to the vocation of someone you admire. However an inclination arises, you only begin to understand its true nature once you pursue it. Over time, you begin to understand the nature of your intended vocation. For instance, you may learn that being a firefighter is more than just saving people from burning buildings. It also entails hours of training, cleaning equipment, and waiting.

Taking classes in school, and later working at different jobs, you gain the perspective necessary to recognize and define your abilities and interests. While it is unlikely that your friend, for example, realized he would one day be a paramedic when he said he wanted to be a fireman, he *knew* he loved helping people. Pursuing his dream of becoming a fireman, Adam realized the true expression of his desires was best channeled through working as a paramedic.

Where to begin if you're unsure about your particular purpose?

Even without looking outside yourself, you can start by taking an inventory of what comes easily to you and what does not: What are your greatest talents? How can those talents be used to provide something others want and need? Which activities do you enjoy the most?

To better focus on the question of identifying your purpose, notice what you are instinctively attracted to and what repels you. In other words, while you may have the capacity to do anything, what would you *prefer* to do? For example, would you rather

- spend time with many people each day or just a few?
- work in one place or travel wherever your work takes you?
- focus on numbers and spreadsheets or words and documents?
- generate novel ideas or organize information?
- confront new challenges daily or spend a lifetime mastering one skill?

Listing your preferences, you are likely to see the outlines of your natural talents. You might notice, for example, that you enjoy analyzing information and are good at it. It would then be helpful to learn this skill is essential in *accounting*, *programming, finance*, and related disciplines. This knowledge might illuminate a number of paths you had not previously considered.

Just notice what *pulls* you in contrast to what you have to *push* yourself to do. For instance, you may notice that you enjoy solving problems on your own, but have to force yourself to give presentations to groups. Conversely, you might realize that you like interacting with strangers and would feel chained down sitting at the same desk in the same office every day. It's important to spend time developing the talent or talents that you enjoy—the activities that draw you onward, body, heart, and mind.

Aligned with your purpose, you naturally feel connected to the best you.

- An aligned body feels strength born from the vitality of creation in motion.
- An aligned heart experiences a deep emotional connection to your work.
- An aligned mind directs itself naturally toward fulfilling your objectives.

Unfortunately, too many of us ignore or postpone the sometimes confusing work of exploration. How do we know we're not being ensnared in *someone else's* notion of what should be or in yesterday's dreams? Distracted from our real purpose, we abdicate our potential. The voice of self-defeat whispers, *I don't know how. I don't have what it takes. I don't deserve it.* But who is holding us back? Why not challenge the limits of what we think we are capable of?

What keeps you from being the real you?

Challenges are easy to put off if they entail risk. For example, once you say, "I'm going to be a firefighter," you commit to running *toward* the fire. You also commit to signing up for and completing rigorous training. Commitment entails the real risk of failure. Maybe you can't carry all your equipment plus the weight of another person over your shoulder down many flights of stairs. Maybe you will not get the job assignment you most desire. Maybe you will complete the training and learn you don't want the job. It takes extraordinary courage to commit your life to your passion openly, to shrug off others' expectations, and to take responsibility for making your dream come true. But what happens if you never try?

For most of us, the greatest challenge of our lives may be identifying our purpose, but our greatest accomplishment is choosing to live into it.

The truth we all come to, sooner or later, is that we can only be ourselves, unique and perfect in our own way. Our distinct perspective contributes to the whole, like a piquant spice in a savory dish or the plaintive sound of a violin floating above the orchestra. Once you fix upon who you are—your true self and your associated purpose—and choose to *live into it*, you will feel it take hold of you. Being the true you is your purpose in life. Choosing that purpose ignites the fire of greatness.

Almost everyone runs *away* from a fire. What fires are you willing to run *toward*?

For Others

Your work is to find out what your work should be and not to neglect it for another's. Clearly discover your work and attend to it with all your heart. —Dhammapada

Who am I to others? So much of who we are is reflected by the people closest to us. As the saying goes, show me your five closest friends, and I will tell you who you are. Those same friends also know you best, in some ways better than you know yourself. When you encounter a long-time friend they will often say, "You look happy," or "You look tired," or "You look as though you're not feeling well." Their impression of you is a source of invaluable feedback.

Friends who know us well and can remain impartial provide the best advice; they see things in us that we can't. We may think we know ourselves well, but how much do we really know? Just consider your outward appearance. How often have you seen your picture and thought, *do I really look like that*? Or heard a recording and been astounded at the sound of your voice? The way we see and hear ourselves in our minds is often very different from objective reality. And then there are our mannerisms, the unconscious tics, gestures, and speech patterns that our friends find endearing and that so surprise us when we are reminded of them.

How might the people closest to you see something more?

Others help us overcome the limitations of our inescapable subjectivity. They help us to uncover overlooked strengths and abilities by directing our attention to what we may not otherwise see. One of the best ways to find out who we are to others is to ask our friends to describe our most basic characteristics. Their responses may be surprising. For example, they may say, "You are so adventurous," even though you consider yourself to be cautious and restrained. Or they may point to character traits you are unaware of. They might say, "You seem happiest when focused on a challenge," suggesting you are fundamentally oriented toward achievement. Those who care and who see objectively will likely discern something unique, something you are unaware of. They may also have a strong sense of the most appropriate course to follow—how you might most profitably spend time. So what do you think your friends or family members would say about you?

Try this: ask five people who know you well the same questions you would ask yourself, plus one that might reveal something new:

- What are my greatest talents?
- How can those talents provide something others want and need?
- In what ways am I holding myself back from reaching my greatest potential?

Let's say, for example, your friends agree that you are a talented painter; you have skillfully reproduced works of great masters. Yet when mentors suggest that you extend the range of your work, you dismiss them. Following a well-trodden path, how far will you get? Not far—your art will seem contrived. The world does not need imitation. What the world wants from each of us is a truthfulness and honesty expressed through our unique point of view. While imitating masters in any medium may increase our understanding of a discipline, greatness ultimately demands that we stand up to be judged on our own merits. Although there will never be another Picasso, other great artists are yet to be revealed.

Why not be among them?

Only by connecting your talents to a purpose will you discover the unique gifts you have to offer the world.

What true purpose does not benefit others?

Living with purpose creates fulfillment and happiness; living a purpose that benefits others provides a platform for greatness, repurposing our true strengths and limitations for others' benefit. Our *greatest selves* are manifested when we harness our talents to serve something greater than ourselves and learn that our vocation, as Aristotle pointed out, lies "where talents and the needs of the world cross." While this may sound like charity, it is not. Everyone has to eat.

Muhammad Ali was a great boxer. He could easily have fought and earned titles only to make money. Hundreds of boxers have had exceptional careers but are little known outside the world of sports. Ali, however, used his ability to box for something more. A controversial and polarizing figure during his time, he used his notoriety to bring attention to the war in Vietnam, to the condition of race relations in America and, later, to the danger of brain injuries associated with contact sports. While he certainly earned a fair sum as a professional fighter, he found his purpose in speaking to causes where he perceived a need. Boxing merely provided the platform to fulfill this purpose.

Ali freed himself from the constraints of just being a successful athlete by asking how he could serve others. Today, he is widely regarded not just for the skills he displayed in the ring but for the values he exemplified outside it. His question is our own: whether to be merely a successful man or a great advocate for mankind.

Considering what we can do or be for others, we extend the range of our capabilities and in so doing, expand what is possible for ourselves. The only limit to our greatness is the scale by which we choose to measure.

For Living Into

The gap between vision and current reality is also a source of energy. If there were no gap, there would be no need for any action to move towards the vision. We call this gap creative tension.
—Peter Senge

The moment we sink our roots into the ground of our environment, intuition springs forth into intentions. *Where* we first take root is less important than *planting* our roots. Action initiates the process. We can always grow in a new direction—and we will when new revelations mandate change. But first we need to establish a place to begin—and from which we grow.

Reflecting on our earlier examples, the initial seeds of our intentions might be to start a business, to extend human life, or to make people laugh. Only through tapping into a particular set of intentions can we determine whether our thoughts, words, and deeds align with our purpose. This assessment begins with self-awareness. Where do we spend our time, money, and energy? Where do we focus our attention? How might our actual allocation of resources conflict with our stated purpose? The more honest we are with ourselves, the more likely we will be able to recognize, react to, and change our behavior until we get it right.

What holds us back from living into our intentions?

Facing our choices, we confront the fear of failure almost immediately. Fear is debilitating, weakening even the most resilient among us, eroding our confidence and compromising the ability to break through the invisible barriers that keep our potential in check. Imagine, for example, that despite dreaming of playing an instrument or painting, you never acted on this desire simply because you believed you were not good enough.

Whenever you have thoughts such as this, just ask yourself what led to these beliefs. Is it possible your attitudes are driven by an ancient fear that has become a story you tell yourself—one you never thought to question? What other evidence do you have that your case is hopeless? Violinists and painters don't just pick up a bow or brush and create an immediate masterpiece. Mastery takes years of practice. But if you deny yourself the opportunity to learn from your mistakes and develop your talent, you forfeit any possibility of success. There is, after all, truth in the timeworn saying: it is better to try and fail than never to try at all.

Begin by taking a calculated risk. Do it *because* it scares you, because it is essential to face it and live into your authentic self. To commit to this experiment is to embark on a wonderful adventure. So long as you postpone this adventure, you may never find what you truly love. Setting the intention to develop your talents will not only be in accord with your purpose; it will be the ultimate expression of your purpose, even as you learn to improve along the way.

There will inevitably be moments of discord when you wonder, *how did I get here? What am I doing with my life?* Be alert to such moments, because they probably indicate you are acting at cross-purposes to your true intentions. If you are willing to face the truth, you will dare to hold your life up to a mirror. And more often than you might imagine, what you see will be surprising. If you stay committed to developing your talents, one day you will look up and find that you actually can play the violin or paint. Conversely, you can almost certainly point to at least one cautionary example of the friend who invested years in an unsatisfying career only to look back one day in utter dismay, recognizing a life wasted fighting an imaginary foe or pursuing someone else's dream.

How do we know when we have lost *our* way? Unbiased feedback from others is good, but it is only half the equation. The other half is to be open to and willing to *act* on the feedback we receive. As we begin to recognize the difference between our potential and actual lives, we become aware of a dissonance in body, heart, and mind—a gap between potential and reality filled with anxiety, disillusionment, and regret. For example, we may say family is the most important thing, only to find ourselves working at our job sixty hours a week. Meanwhile, birthday parties, soccer games, and piano recitals pass by without us.

The good news is that this gap also drives us toward resolution. In other words, it provides a creative tension, energy to harness for the benefit of making necessary change. If you want to play the violin well, the desire to close the gap between your *vision* (playing beautiful music) and *current reality* (shrieking sounds that cause the neighbor's dog to howl) creates tension and energy. You sign up for lessons; you critique your performance, practice, and expend real energy to achieve your goal.

And what if you discover that you don't really like playing the violin? Sometimes the gap illuminates what we have concealed from ourselves or confronts us with a reality we have denied. Maybe your parents are avid musicians and you feel pressured to be the same. The gap, however, reinforces the need to align your intentions with your natural way of being. In this case, it may mean accepting that you are "musically challenged." Beating yourself up when you're not completely aligned accomplishes nothing; forcing yourself to keep taking violin lessons even when you find no pleasure in learning to play only makes you miserable and wastes time and money.

Once we identify the gap, how do we close it?

We know we're on our true path when we feel vital and happy. As vision, words, and actions align, we feel the flow of positive energy of living into what we are capable of, and this growing happiness brightens the lives of people around us. And once we are on the right course, if we are truly passionate about what we are committed to, there can be enjoyment even in the effort.

Aligning to your commitments is a practice, even if you never entirely succeed in eliminating the gap. With practice, you progress. Any missteps merely help distinguish the path to success. Even the masters never cease trying to improve. They just learn to enjoy the journey. In the end, you really have no choice but to give yourself over to the fulfillment of your purpose, though its realization may take more than a lifetime. Greatness is not about succeeding; rather, it's about choosing to be the best *you* through every thought, word, and action in service of something greater than yourself.

Chapter 1 Summary: *Who Am I?* invites us to examine the domain of self

Just as each of us is physically different, we each have a unique purpose, even if it overlaps with that of others. No two violinists play exactly the same way. A purpose need not be a lofty goal; a purpose connects the intuitive (what is) with the intentional (what is possible). The highest expression of our purpose brings forward our natural talents for the benefit of others—not merely in doing what we are good at but what makes us feel alive. And living into our purpose, directly and indirectly, contributes to our happiness and the happiness of others. Should we fail to live into our purpose, on the other hand, we are destined to a life of nagging dissatisfaction.

From the perspective of *self*, purpose appears where responses to these three questions intersect:

1. What are my greatest talents?
2. How can they be used to provide something others want and need?
3. Which of these activities do I most enjoy?

From the perspective of our relationships with *others*, taking advantage of their objective feedback can be helpful. Others' insights can be invaluable; often, they see potential within us that we are unable to see. They are not burdened with the stories we tell ourselves that distort or damage our confidence and have us believe we are incomplete.

- How might those closest to you see something more?
- How do you hold yourself back from reaching your greatest potential?
- What is a true purpose that does *not* benefit others?

From the perspective of *living into* our purpose, the gap between status quo and what we are capable of creates useful tension. When we are living into our purpose, we feel vital and engaged, the tension propelling us toward what is possible. When we resist, the tension compounds frustration and discontent. However, until we are willing to try, and face the risk of failing, we cannot realize our greatest potential. Failure is merely the seal of an authentic challenge.

- What holds you back from living into your intentions?
- How do you know when you have lost your way?
- Once you identify the gap, how can you close it?

CHAPTER 2. HOW DO I IMPACT OTHERS?

I've learned that people will forget what you said, people will forget what you did, but people will never forget how you made them feel. —Maya Angelou

How do I impact others? The following story illuminates how a small, seemingly insignificant gesture has the power to change someone's life.

Consider Robert, a successful businessman who runs his own company. Robert grew up in a tough part of New York City. Like the other teenagers he knew, he joined a gang. Robert's gang was fierce and traveled as a pack, hustling and intimidating everyone in their path. One day they were together in a subway car, each clad in a black leather jacket, combat boots, and torn clothing bristling with metal studs. Mingling with his friends, Robert noticed a man in a suit at the other end of the car: a typical businessman—an easy mark for the gang if they chose to make him one. Robert decided Mr. Businessman needed to show some respect. Edging away from his friends, he bore down on the guy with a fuck-you stare, jaw clenched, eyes steeled. This was *their* subway car.

The man looked back but didn't budge. The car kept traveling down the tracks. Robert moved closer, like a predator sizing up his prey, his aura of menace magnified by the pack at his back. The man still did not move to the next car.

Half listening to Tony, one of his crew, recounting a story, Robert was approaching the decisive moment when he would be compelled to back up his bluff and pounce on Mr. Businessman like a coiled spring unloading. At that moment, Tony closed his tale with ". . . and then I kicked him in the face!" Everyone laughed conspiratorially, and Robert, distracted, fell back into conversation with his crew.

A few stops went by, and the businessman rose from his seat to exit, catching Robert's attention. As he stepped from the car, he looked back at Robert and gave him a kind smile and a nod, the sort of nod of affirmation you would extend to a friend across a crowded room. Robert couldn't believe it—in the face of all his hostility, the man had extended a caring gesture without hope of its being returned. The businessman disappeared into the station, and Robert never saw him again.

But the man made an impression. Robert couldn't understand how this guy could be nice to him in the face of so much hostility. What was the man acknowledging—was it something about Robert or about the man's own way of being? Robert never did find an answer to that question and continued to wonder about the man whose glance soon caused the seed of kindness to germinate within him.

Shortly after the event in the subway car, Robert cut his hair, put on a button-down shirt, and set out to find a job. Someone took a chance on him and he worked hard. Although Robert often felt the lure of the streets, he kept on the straight and narrow, one day at a time. Not so many years after that crucial first job, with a little luck and a lot of perseverance, Robert started his own company.

Today, the tattoos are mostly covered by long sleeves, the chains and studs are gone, and the leather jacket is Italian. The vestige of Robert that was part of the gang is still there, but the Robert who chose to cultivate the kindness another human being recognized in him is now running a growing business. Nowadays, if you should meet him, you will find you can't help being affected by his smile. It is as warm as the sun.

Who we are isn't unchanging. The seeds of possibility are inside each of us. Whether they germinate depends, in part, on our environment and the attitudes and judgments of those closest to us—loam and fertilizer to our potential. If negative feedback compacts the soil and the seedlings are offered no encouragement, they cannot take root and grow.

Of course, we impact the self-image and prospects of others just as they impact ours. The things we think, say, and do, and even our mere physical presence, influence the people in our lives positively or negatively in ways often unforeseen. With greater awareness, we can be more deliberate in bringing out the best in ourselves and in the people around us. Properly receptive to the opportunities, we find no shortage of seeds to nurture. Just as we absorb the nutrients from our environment, our thoughts, words, and actions have the power to sustain, even transform, the lives of those around us.

Looking at the man on the train, Robert saw him as a thug would see him: someone to bully or take advantage of, because that is likely how Robert was treated by his own gang when he was an outsider. It probably reflected his own fear of being rejected by his gang. Robert treated others harshly to demonstrate that he embodied the gang's ethos, reinforcing his feeling of belonging. In the same way, the man on the train could have chosen to think of Robert as nothing more than a troublemaker—whispered a warning to his seatmate, averted his eyes, and formulated a quick escape plan. Instead, he had the presence and confidence to be himself. In the end, his confidence and compassion short-circuited Robert's expectations, making an indelible and transformative impression.

In light of the inescapable effects of human interaction, it helps to consider the following as we meet others:

- What is my body communicating?
- Are my words true and helpful?
- What are my thoughts promoting?

It is also important to be aware of our motivations. Which is to say, we should be mindful of whether we are seeking something from our interaction or are simply offering ourselves freely, hoping only to share the moment and be a positive force.

For My Self

[For] every living being . . . seemingly affected only by its immediate surrounding, the sphere of external influence extends to infinite distance. —Nikola Tesla

Take a moment and evaluate yourself. On a scale of 1 to 10 (1 being the lowest and 10 being the highest), grade your own appearance, capacity for empathy, and intelligence. How would you rate yourself in the following respects?

Appearance: _____ [1-10]
Empathy: _____ [1-10]
Intelligence: _____ [1-10]

Now ask yourself how you arrived at these results: What analysis did you make? How do others' opinions influence your own?

More likely than not, the ratings you assigned to yourself were based, consciously or unconsciously, on reflections of the way others have responded to you or your view of your relative rank within a given community. For example, your perception of your intellect is probably partly based on scores from tests you have taken, the grades you earned in school, or your place within the hierarchy at work, each reflective of performance in a narrow range of endeavor. But comparing yourself to others may not fully reveal what you are capable of, just as others' comparisons can potentially undermine your willingness to risk trying.

Other people, particularly their judgments, can influence our perception of reality. And sometimes, we negatively interpret what others say:

"Maybe you need new glasses." (*My eyes are going bad.*)
"Have you spoken to your mother lately?"(*No. I must be a terrible child.*)
"Maybe you need a tutor for algebra." (*I can't do math.*)

Given the almost infinite number of opportunities for misunderstanding or misinterpreting the things others tell us about ourselves, it is important to reserve a very healthy skepticism for the self-image we carry around. (What does your voice of wisdom say about this image?) It helps to refrain from acting on or reacting to any reflexive assumptions you might be making about what they say or do.

Consider how often the feedback we receive is fundamentally a reflection of someone else's current frame of mind, with no reference whatever to us—such as when we read our friend's distracted brooding over his personal problems as disapproval of what we're saying. Think of how hard it is to sift fact from fiction, even when we are aware someone has spoken maliciously. Finally, consider the all-too-human tendency to overgeneralize and to overemphasize. How complicated! In light of this and a hundred similar considerations, the only truly meaningful measure of any aspect of your being comes from within. Just ask: *Am I being my best self?* Whenever we base our worth on others' preferences, we risk becoming addicted to that approval and distanced from our own values.

After identifying the numerous ways others have impacted our lives, it helps to remember we have the same effect on them. How we see others—the way we hold them in our minds, what we say to them, and even what our bodies express—also influences how they perceive themselves.

Our actions reflect the truth—or lack of truth—of our words. We may say something is important but rush to move past it. Perhaps we think we are open to an idea, but fold our arms across our chests and close off our bodies. We say we respect someone and their ideas, yet purse our lips in disbelief as we listen to them, or worse yet, roll our eyes.

What is your body saying right now?

Imagine you are having a conversation with someone you love right now. What are you doing as you talk? Are you smiling or frowning? As they speak, do you draw closer or lean away? When you say, "I love you," are you looking into her eyes or turning away? Any inconsistency between words and actions leaves us confused or uneasy: *Why did he say he loves me*, she wonders, *when he won't look me in the eye?*

Just as your words do, your body telegraphs your state of mind. The way you stand or sit or cross your arms adds a visceral subtext to what you are saying.

Even without the benefit of words or tone, we interpret conversations we can't hear merely by observing gestures.

Often, we divine the nature of a conversation simply by observing the mannerisms accompanying it—a smile of interest, a furrowed brow of concern, a widening of enthusiastic eyes. In a glance, we intuit people's interests and the subtle messages behind their words. The same is true of our own demeanor. Imagine how others might respond if you were to walk into a room with shoulders slumped forward, face tense, and mouth pursed. Now imagine walking in with shoulders back, face relaxed, and smiling. It's easy to envision how people might interact with you differently depending on your disposition.

What we often forget is that our physical state also affects what we hear. With your arms crossed or face averted, your capacity to listen is compromised. What might you be avoiding or shielding yourself from? Examining your attitude in such moments, you may realize you are limiting your perception.

How might we become more intentional with what our bodies are communicating? Imagine approaching a conversation with a relaxed and open posture. Aligning yourself in a natural state of receptivity is like adjusting the tuner on a radio. It enhances your ability to transmit and receive with greater clarity, helping you to gain a more complete understanding of the message between the words.

Increasing the congruence between your actions and your words, you convey acceptance and trust. When your message is coupled with the right intentions, the waves ripple forth. As we learned from the businessman who affirmed Robert's potential for goodness in the face of overt hostility, even the smallest gesture can have a profound impact on someone's life.

For Others

There exists, for everyone, a sentence—a series of words—that has the power to destroy you. Another sentence exists, another series of words, that could heal you. —Philip K. Dick

The strength of any relationship is measurable by the range of topics open to discussion. In the strongest relationships, we can talk about anything without fear of repercussion. But an absence of care, curiosity, or commitment produces an undercurrent of questionable motives. Recognizing the influence of our speech, we must always be aware of how our words affect other people. Are we co-creating an objective and compassionate environment? Everything we say builds or erodes trust, reflects emotional connection or distance, and expands or contracts choice.

How important are the right words?

The words we choose have the potential to create different realities—to birth nations, give form to our intentions, and set people in motion. They are a form of energy that flows from us to the people we meet, and to others we may never know.

Words help illuminate truths we are blind to. However, if words are malicious or misplaced, they can push us further into darkness and damage our lives in a thousand ways. The most hurtful words are sweeping, unspecific valuations made by those closest to us. We can easily ignore many things people say to us, particularly if there is no reasonable basis for them or when a complete stranger says them. If, for example, a passerby comments that you look like a blue kangaroo, it has little effect; a quick glance in the mirror confirms that you are neither blue nor a kangaroo. But if your mother repeatedly says, "You should be more like your sister" or "Nobody cares what you think," her words have the power to infect like a virus. We are all vulnerable to the opinions of others, particularly those of people we care about most and respect.

Each of us carries around the memories of things said to us years ago that we still consider true today. The potential we see within ourselves is partly a social construct, the product of how others have spoken or acted toward us until we mistake *their* behavior for who *we* are. A history of harsh and demeaning words can leave a legacy of immeasurable anxiety and self-doubt. How many people spend their lives seeking approval in one way or another? By comparison, almost all the happiest and most successful people have had someone tell them, over and over until they believed it, things like, "If you have the talent and work hard enough, you can do whatever you set your mind to," or "I will always love you, no matter what." Words of encouragement, spoken with conviction, give rise to a healthy confidence that naturally flows from unconditional acceptance. Directly or indirectly, they influence a lifetime of choices.

How do we measure the wisdom of our words?

The test of the wisdom of our speech can be reduced to three elements: Is it true? Is it helpful? And, can it be heard? Being honest and sincere in word and deed builds trust, reinforcing the bond of loyalty between two people. If our words offer something of value or, at a minimum, are positive, we are probably speaking wisely. When we catch ourselves being deceitful, impolite, or humiliating, we should wonder whether we're being driven by our fears and insecurities. Lies are poison. And truth unchecked by compassion can lead to cruelty.

When we speak with honesty in a way that promotes harmony and goodwill, communication serves to further our understanding of ourselves and others, consistent with our intentions. Moreover, we should never forget that we can't truly communicate with someone until we know what is important to them and can phrase our thoughts in ways that are meaningful. Knowing this, we instinctively attribute sincerity and wisdom to someone who listens intently and speaks deliberately (and vice versa).

What are we communicating in the silence between us?

We enhance communication when we intentionally invite silence into the conversation. Where else do we evaluate our choices or form our bonds? Put another way, the quality of silence between our words is as important as what we say. These silent interludes often shape our experience—how we make meaning, whether we feel comfortable and relaxed, charged with curiosity, or agitated before we speak.

Just notice the current of any conversation—the natural back-and-forth flow of the energy between two people. With some people, it is impossible to resist the impulse to fill the silence with words. The quiet feels awkward. With others, it is a pleasure to relax into the space of silence. With still others, even the briefest pause provides the opportunity to study ourselves: What have we chosen to say or not say? What still needs to be said?

This oscillation creates a sympathetic rhythm between speaker and listener that deepens dialogue and promotes real sharing. Like the rests between the notes of a melody, the pauses between utterances in a conversation create a harmonic exchange.

For Living Into

Those who bring sunshine to the lives of others cannot keep it from themselves. —James Matthew Barrie

What are we bringing forth in others? We all have the ability to see the beauty, truth, and goodness that exist in virtually everyone we encounter. The people we meet are more than just their roles, another series of bullets on our agenda.

Seeing people in stereotypical or self-involved ways obscures the fullness of humanity. Why do we reduce whole lives to a series of snapshots—some of them flattering, some not? It takes courage to deepen our inquiry until we illuminate the common threads of our existence. But approaching everyone we meet this way reveals the vividness of human life.

Consider the following scenario: It's the end of the day and you're eager to get home. In the elevator, you encounter the lady who cleans the building, just starting her workday. Most days you might not even say hello to her, justifying your indifference with the excuse that she probably doesn't want to be bothered or doesn't speak English. You might not think of her as a person at all, but merely as the embodiment of a utilitarian function.

But what if you took a moment to see her apart from the work she does? What if you took the time to acknowledge her qualities as a human being: body, heart, and mind? You might notice her dignified posture, kind eyes, or warm smile. Maybe you notice a piece of jewelry and imagine the occasion when someone she loves gave it to her. Perhaps you feel an emotional connection and empathize with her, seeing how hard she works without complaint to create a better life for herself or her family.

If you allow yourself to relate to the cleaning lady in this way, it is only a short step to realizing that everyone is far more than their societal position, and that each person has their own wisdom. The cleaning lady is far more than her job. She is a person with her own unique expression of grace, positivity, and wisdom. Allowing ourselves to see the full humanity of the cleaning lady—or the police officer or bank teller—we are on our way to seeing every person we meet the same way, as a fully realized human being and a potential friend.

How does our treatment of others reflect our maturity?

It is easy to label people and confine them to the roles we ascribe to them. Acknowledging others as they are instead of viewing them as characters within your story is a skill to practice. It requires awareness to resist the impulse to dismiss someone as "just a salesman," or "just a cleaning lady," or *just* anything. But when we submit to the moment and acknowledge the real human beings in front of us, we suddenly realize they are more than just their roles, that they—just like our closest neighbors, our parents, or our grandparents—have rich, abundant lives that have nothing to do with us. In the instant we see our father as the young man whose heart was broken by a beautiful girl we'll never meet, we change; our universe suddenly adds a dimension or two and we feel a new intimacy with that mysterious man who raised us.

We often fail to realize that we can choose to enrich our environment by responding to people as individuals. Part of the difficulty is resisting the temptation to treat others as shabbily as we sometimes feel treated. An important aspect of being our better selves consists in choosing to respond to the better self in everyone we meet.

Noticing and acknowledging the best in others in ways they can hear and understand liberates beauty, truth, and goodness. Adding positive thoughts, words, and gestures, we amplify our influence. In bringing out the best in the people we meet, we naturally bring out the best in ourselves. Thus, the golden rule has a corollary: how we do unto *others* is how we do unto *ourselves*.

Chapter 2 Summary: *How Do We Impact Others?* invites us to examine the domain of others

We all leave a wake, intentionally or unintentionally; even the smallest gesture or comment made in passing can have a profound influence lasting a lifetime. *How* we communicate and *what* messages we send are as vital as the words we choose. Meaning is imparted through physical expression as well as the rhythm and tone of our speech. The right messages provide inspiration and the opportunity for growth.

From the perspective of *self*, our self-image consists, in part, of a mosaic of other people's subjective opinions and perceptions. It's important to understand that what people communicate often reflects more about their perspectives and insecurities than about the true nature of the recipient. The first step toward recognizing the impact we have on others is to be aware of our physical expressions. Words do not exist in a vacuum.

- How do *others'* opinions impact your life?
- What is your body saying right now?
- How can you be intentional with what your body communicates?

From the perspective of our relationships with *others*, the message is similar. The wisdom of our speech can best be measured by its veracity and influence. Before speaking, pass your words through these gates: *Are they true? Are they helpful?* Words of acknowledgment encourage; thoughtless opinions discourage. Remember also that the best way to be heard is to listen. Silence allows us to digest meaning, offers the opportunity to evaluate the message, and opens space for revelation.

- How important are the right words?
- How can you measure the wisdom of your words?
- What are *we* communicating in the *silence between us*?

From the perspective of *living into* our relationships with others, it's critical to remember that when we compartmentalize people, we strip them of humanity and drain our own lives of richness and depth. Recognizing beauty, truth, and goodness in everyone we encounter liberates potential— theirs and ours.

- How do your thoughts, words, and actions influence the potential in others?
- How is your maturity reflected in the way you treat others?
- What arises when you promote beauty, truth, and goodness?

CHAPTER 3. HOW WILL I SPEND THIS DAY?

This is the beginning of a new day. I have been given this day to use as I will. I can waste it or use it for good, but what I do today is important because I am exchanging a day of my life for it. When tomorrow comes, this day will be gone forever, leaving in its place something that I have traded for it. —Ric Kausrud

One day. Twenty-four hours, 1,440 minutes, 86,400 seconds; the time it takes the earth to rotate around its axis; the interval of life in which your heart ticks off another 100,000 beats. What better unit of time to mark the natural rhythm of our conscious lives? Unlike other units of time, a single day is crisp and comprehensible, clearly marked with a beginning, a middle, and an end.

In a fraction of a day, we can climb a mountain, run a marathon, or fly halfway around the world. We can read a book from beginning to end, prepare a wonderful dinner and invite all our friends, or teach a child a valuable skill that will serve her for a lifetime.

While we often envision our lives in terms of months or years, almost every milestone in our lives can be mapped to a single day. The moments captured within each one forever mark our lives as they irrevocably change our perception of the future: birthdays, weddings, and holidays; the day you first wobbled down the sidewalk on your training wheels; and the day you hung your bike in the garage at the end of the last unclaimed summer of childhood. The day you began your first job and felt the thrill of possibilities, or the day you packed up your belongings as you said your final goodbye. There are also the unplanned events that alter the course of our lives: the day you met your soulmate or the day you received shocking news from a routine medical examination. Days you wanted to go on forever, and days so painful they couldn't end soon enough.

Although these watershed events account for only a tiny fraction of your life, they are transcendent moments of change. You live most of your life, however, in the space *between* these milestones. The way you choose to live each day often determines the rate of attaining the goals you set and, sometimes, the nature and frequency of the milestones that befall you.

If you keep a daily journal or a day planner, pull it out and review the events of the past week. If you don't keep a journal, take a moment to memorialize just one day from the recent past. If today is a Tuesday, think back to last Tuesday, seven short days ago. Without your journal or day planner or some dated record, can you even remember what happened a week ago?

As the events of last Tuesday emerge in your mind, ask yourself these questions and write the responses in a journal:

1. How did I spend my time?
2. What was I most excited about?
3. What was I most worried about?

Now review your notes. Of the issues that consumed your time and attention a week ago, how many of the pressing concerns are still important today? In other words, how much energy did you deliberately devote toward reaching your objectives, and how much energy did you exhaust reacting to the random exigencies of the day?

More likely than not, last week's priorities are old news; what was frustrating, thrilling, or frightening a week ago is now a memory consigned to the appropriate category in your storehouse of experience. Even unresolved issues probably evoke less emotion now than they did at the time. Today is a different story, driven by a fresh set of urgent projects, worries, and rewards.

We all want to feel that our time contributes to something meaningful, that the net result of our days brings us closer to the goals that define our purpose. Yet all too frequently we feel as though our days spend us. We get up and go to work, we struggle to meet a deadline, we join a friend for lunch, we go back to work and keep at it past closing time, we stop by the store to grab dinner, and then we find a way to entertain ourselves until we shuffle off to bed. *Where did the time go?*

Despite the parade of days that all look the same, we end each day hoping to wake up and discover a better life. Then we find ourselves doing the same thing we did yesterday, no closer to the life we want. Rather than building toward our goals, we feel trapped in a numbing cycle of sameness, robotically going through the motions of life without meaning.

In hindsight, it is usually fairly easy to see which actions advanced our goals and how much time we've simply squandered. Too often we spend hours wantonly, each like another dollar from a dwindling roll in our pocket, until we realize with a start that our wallet is empty and wonder where the day went.

In fact, it is instructive to consider time in an economic sense, as a kind of existential currency exchanged like a dollar, peso, or yen. Each day subtracts from the balance. As the days, weeks, and years pass, it's hard not to ask whether we are burning through the currency of our lives and to feel some measure of regret.

The voice of regret has a purpose: it fuels the desire to make the most of each day, to consume the last drop of nourishment from our experience. When we lose focus and unwittingly waste our time, the voice of regret reminds us that each precious day can be lived only once, because time is irreplaceable. In ignoring this voice, we run the risk of exhausting our energy to no purpose. But in stopping, truly listening, and awakening to the present, we can regain focus and simply begin again, living the life we consciously choose.

How we spend this day will determine how we spend our lives. We are all trading our lives for something. What are you trading yours for?

For My Self

If you limit your choices only to what seems possible or reasonable, you disconnect yourself from what you truly want, and all that is left is compromise. —Robert Fritz

Let's start over. Blank slate. *Tabula rasa.* You wake up in the morning. Today is a new day, a day to be savored or saved. Beside your bed on the table is a sheet of paper and a pencil. Printed across the top of the sheet is one question: "How will I *invest* this day?"

Before committing to something, you might first ask the following questions:

- What is on my must-do list for today?
- What else can I do to advance my long-term goals?
- How can I approach each task with equanimity?

First start with what *must* get done. List only the truly essential tasks. On an ordinary day, these might include eating, sleeping, and going to school or work. Although it may seem that the musts take up an entire day, a closer inspection will reveal this is not so. Granted, everyone must eat well, sleep well, and find the best way of earning the wherewithal to pay the rent. But even the busiest days are full of interludes between chores that, over the course of the day, can accommodate a dozen elective activities—things like stopping for a coffee or tea or catching up on the daily news. If you consider these free periods, you might realize that considerable time is taken up with distractions unrelated to your long-term goals. Giving in to distractions, you relegate the hope of attaining success, significance, or satisfaction to an indefinite future: *I'll begin the path toward greatness . . . tomorrow.*

In looking more carefully at how and where you spend your time, recognize that what you are doing reflects your values and priorities. For example, you might choose to work a few extra hours or leave a bit early to spend time with someone you care about. Some things may be on your list only because they are necessary steps toward a specific objective: You might choose to invest time in your job to earn the lucrative promotion that will provide a better lifestyle. Putting in the extra hours is a trade-off you are willing to make.

How can we learn to invest our time?

Given the value of each day, ask yourself if you are choosing to *invest* the days in meaningful ways or simply allowing them to be consumed with little to show for your time. Although investing is not always superior to consuming, every investment we make today offers the prospect of dividends tomorrow. Using dollars as an analogy for time, let a day be equal to a hundred dollars. You can go to the store and spend it all on clothes and gadgets or deposit the money in a bank where it will draw interest and increase in value. Or you might choose to strike a balance between saving and spending by investing the money so you can take a longer and better vacation a year from now.

While clear, long-term objectives are essential, without a roadmap, it's easy to lose focus; the Big Picture is hard to track over weeks and months filled with complications and surprises. With no map to help us find our way, the milestones become a series of receding mirages on the horizon.

How can you spend time doing exactly what you choose?

When people say they want to be happy, sometimes what they mean is that they want to do *whatever* they want, *whenever* they want, the world bending to their will. But that's like saying we want the sky to be sunny and cloud-free every day. We can't control the weather any more than we can control the people in our environment or our place in history.

But even in the most highly regimented of routines, such as when we're at school or work, we still have a large degree of choice. We can almost always find a way to enjoy our work. For example, we might profit from a change of venue, choosing to write that report on a sunny park bench instead of in a stuffy cubicle on the twentieth floor. We can choose a more simpatico co-worker and team up with someone who pushes us to improve or makes us laugh. Or we might simply play a game—try to break a record and set some personal best. Even if the work itself is truly unpleasant, we can choose to focus on the rewards of doing it well—and on the promise of a vacation, a bonus, a promotion, or maybe even just keeping a roof over our heads. Happiness is always available when we remember to devote our full attention to being *present* to whatever we choose to focus on.

At a minimum, it is helpful to be mindful of whether we are conscious of our choices. To be sure, each choice has consequences, but nonetheless, we do have these choices. How we choose to spend time will influence the gap between the life we are living and the life we want. The gap will shrink, persist, or expand depending on what we choose.

For Others

If you want to build a ship, don't drum up people to collect wood and don't assign them tasks and work, but rather teach them to long for the endless immensity of the sea. —Antoine de Saint-Exupéry

How much more can we accomplish working together? When we use clichés about "team spirit" or "chemistry," we're talking about something rare but real. Two or more people working harmoniously in furtherance of a shared transcendent purpose have the power to catalyze a chain reaction of inspiration and creative effort approaching magic. When selfish interest is subordinated to the common good in an atmosphere of collective sacrifice, one plus one is more than two.[4]

Team sports provide excellent examples of how human beings devoted to achieving a shared and deeply felt goal are capable of astounding feats. Consider a professional baseball, basketball, or football team that regularly wins championships. It's easy to attribute such success to a star athlete, but how well would even the most promising athlete play without supportive teammates, a motivating coach, and dedicated fans?

Physical skill alone is not enough; the critical factor is leadership. What distinguishes a merely talented athlete from a great one is the ability to draw out the very best in others. Such leaders arouse the passion that inspires teammates to give 110 percent, day in and day out. Great leaders ensure that everyone around them knows they are are a valued member of a successful team on an inspiring mission—promoting a culture of collaboration where all are aligned, and where individual rewards are proportional to collective success. In this atmosphere, it is easier for everyone to set egos aside and stay focused on the common objective, leading or following as the situation calls for. Even a star has to adhere to the game plan and complement the initiatives of other team members. Teammates on such teams help each other achieve greatness.

What inspires you to put your heart into your work?

Simply reflect on your experience: Are you willing to put your heart into a project that doesn't inspire you? It's easy to assume that people are motivated only by personal gain, but most of us will work only so long and so hard for money alone. Although it is true that some relationships are built on financial ties, the promise of financial success alone can never kindle the inspiration necessary to summon our best. The heart of a seamlessly effective team is a shared commitment to achieving a higher goal.

Think about teams such as the New York Yankees or Manchester United that have spent hundreds of millions of dollars in an effort to buy a championship. Despite signing the most talented athletes for each position on the team, they often fail to win, even with their gold-plated staff. Such teams may even include a player who is among the best in the world, a charismatic physical genius. And still the team fails to make the playoffs. Sports teams packed with hand-picked, lavishly paid stars, even teams with truly legendary players, risk failing so long as they are built around the ideal of individual over team.

What unites a high-performance team?

The same purposeful, coordinated teamwork seen in sports dynasties can be observed all around us. The local fire and police departments, actors putting on a stage production, the cooks and waitstaff at your favorite restaurant all rely on the coordination of finely tuned teams. Think of the various teams you have been part of. What was it about the best teams that made them successful, and why did the unsuccessful teams fail?

Whether you're the star, a supporting player, a coach, or a fan, the other people in your life contribute to your success—just as you contribute to theirs. We all recognize that we are not our normal selves when we do our very best work—that we are somehow inspired. By being present and alert, being responsive to others, and having an intuitive awareness of how and where our efforts support the unfolding of the whole, we produce work from the heart. And when our hearts feel committed to an inspiring vision, what are we not capable of?

For Living Into

The sun's rays do not burn until brought to a focus. —*Alexander Graham Bell*

How many times a day are you hijacked by things that don't really matter? Assume you have determined how to make the best use of your time and created goals that inspire others to collaborate with you. How do you remain focused and prevent irrelevant distractions from diverting your team from its purpose?

Inevitably, you'll face a mix of essential and nonessential tasks that will overwhelm any schedule, always being left with the problem of how to allocate your time, energy, and resources productively. Consider the power of saying no, or more specifically, saying yes to less. Every time you say yes to something that is unrelated to your goals, you are saying no to your goals. Staying on course requires ruthless prioritization.

A well-known businessman once described the secret to his success: On any given day he is likely to be presented with twenty new opportunities to invest his time or money. His job, he said, is to say no to at least twenty-one of them. He was kidding, of course, but still making the point that the prosperity of his business improves each time he says no.

Returning to the example of the events of last Tuesday, consider how many seemingly urgent tasks actually con-tributed to your long-term goals. If you were engaged with even a single activity that brought a major goal nearer to fruition, you were ahead of the game. However, it helps to remember that it is within your power to make incremental progress on major objectives almost every day. All that is required is taking ownership of how you allocate time, keeping goals in mind and seizing any opportunity that presents itself—and being willing to say no to those things that impede progress and offer no new perspective.

One of those common phrases whose meaning is not always clear is "a job well done." How do we know when we're doing something well? Fully engaged in a task, we experience an optimal skill/challenge ratio accompanied by a pleasurable harmony among thoughts, emotions, and physical activities—the challenge of the moment eliciting our utmost efforts and highest levels of skill. In the field of athletics, this harmony of mind and body has been described as "being in the flow" or what we might call a "state of harmonic flow."

We all know this state of flow—episodes of becoming so involved in an activity that we lose track of time and temporarily forget who and where we are. We often experience the flow playing sports, listening to music, or working on an engaging project as the rest of the world falls away and a feeling of ease and contentment sets in. Engaged in the vividness of the moment, we become hyperconnected to the object of our awareness and oblivious to everything else. These are the *moments of being* we live for, when we realize the full richness of life.

Mindfulness

Here, it might be valuable to touch on how mindfulness provides access to harmonic flow, even in the midst of boring or mundane tasks. With apologies to all the teachers and practitioners of the hundreds (if not thousands) of forms of mindfulness, let us describe mindfulness as a process of steadying the mind. It is the delicate state that precedes thinking, unconstrained by comparison, reflection, or analysis. It is a practice of nonegoic, total awareness in the present moment—the raw, unfiltered connection to the here and now, free from attachment to thought. In such a state, habits are unable to form. Experiences arise as if happening for the first time.

While there are many good resources for learning the practice of mindfulness, it may be helpful to understand what it is and why it is so important. Using various techniques, we can learn to adopt an awareness of awareness itself; once freed from compulsive thoughts, we are better able to focus outward and become present to our environment. In an advanced state of continuous and profound awareness, we choose where to place our attention: Where is it needed most? Attaining such a degree of clarity helps us make the wisest use of our attention as we pursue our long-term goals.

But even though we often hear of mindfulness, relatively few spend much time *practicing* being mindful. Why is this? The most frequent excuse is lack of time, but this is just a rationalization. There is actually plenty of time to cultivate mindfulness—to meditate—even in the midst of a thoroughly modern life. Many contemporary urban dwellers learn to meditate while driving or taking a train or bus to work, while standing in line, or whenever they find themselves waiting for someone or something. What better use to make of idle interludes?

With practice, mindfulness grounds us in our environment, promotes equanimity, and dampens the chattering of the voices in our head, intensifying the ability to focus. These are essentially the characteristics of a state of harmonic flow and describe the state mindfulness masters are in most of the time.

How is happiness linked to success?

Achieving wholeness—harmony and satisfaction in all life's domains—requires a healthy balance. Devoting all your energy to one domain of life while neglecting others for prolonged periods leads to an imbalance. Happiness need not be deferred. Being on the right path, embodying your purpose, gives rise to a growing sense of fulfillment. While goals provide a focal point, happiness is not strictly about achieving a goal or any combination of goals.

Happiness can also come about when you become immune to short-term disappointments. Instead of focusing exclusively on the goal of the day, invest in all areas of your life: in health, relationships, finances, learning, and spiritual growth. Although such investments take time to mature, they inspire the confidence that you have invested time and effort wisely, making it easier to ignore daily fluctuations and temporary setbacks.

By choosing a course that resonates within us, what Carlos Castaneda called a "path with heart," and by giving ourselves to every twist and turn along the way, we create the optimal conditions for a healthy state of flow in our daily lives. When this happens, any difficulties and setbacks are transformed from petty distractions into reminders, rituals, and milestones marking our progress.

Just as Lao Tzu wrote, "A journey of ten thousand miles starts with a single step," each day presents us with a series of individual steps. Your task is to ensure that each step brings you closer to your goal, even if it seems far beyond reach. Therefore, in choosing how to spend *this* day, be mindful of your goals to ensure you're moving in the right direction.

When we take a moment and become present to the life we have been given, how can we help but be filled with inspiration? In these moments of wonder, like children visiting the circus for the first time, we delight in the vivid spectacle of incredible feats of strength, courage, and agility taking place all around us.

What will you do today with your one-day pass to the greatest show on earth?

Chapter 3 Summary: *How Will I Spend This Day?* invites us to examine the domain of the future

Days are a natural, workable measure for charting the course of our lives. Almost every significant event in our history can be traced back to a particular day. While we often idealize the future or fret over the past, in reality, we have only *this* day. Each one is precious, and a happy and purposeful life requires a careful investment of our time, though many of us do not fully appreciate its value until it is gone.

When you honestly examine how you spend your days, you realize that

- even a day filled with obligations permits time to practice living into your intentions;
- while you cannot always choose your environment, you are free to adopt a healthy attitude toward any environment; and
- when you choose to do anything well, you find contentment in doing it.

Finally, success depends on setting and achieving goals *each day*. We can commit ourselves to the next point along our path and if we achieve nothing else, learn from our mistakes. Or we can lose focus, be lured away by diversions, and wonder where the time goes as it slips away.

From the perspective of *self*, it is illuminating to discover how much of what we do is inessential. Once we understand how much of our day is actually available to us, we can purposefully choose how we invest or consume it. Otherwise, compulsively responding to demands that are not aligned with our objectives, we fail to advance long-term goals. We need to ignore distractions and seize the unclaimed time already available to us.

- What will you accomplish today to advance your long-term goals?
- What are you willing to give (or give up) to succeed?
- What experiences would you like to create in the process?

From the perspective of our relationships with *others*, making the most of each day requires collaboration. By articulating mutually beneficial ideals, we create the foundation for partnership. In concert, a team can accomplish something greater than the sum of its parts.

- How can you leverage your time as well as others'?
- How does collaboration lead to success?
- What are the elements of a true partnership?

From the perspective of *living into* this day, it is worth remembering that success depends on distinguishing the merely urgent from the important. Few matters that seem urgent are truly as important as we first perceive them to be. Doing a few things well is more effective than overcommitting and accomplishing little. By concentrating on the task at hand, we can generate enthusiasm. Mindfulness helps us focus, calms us, and draws us into the flow. A sustained state of harmonic flow is a catalyst for success. Consider the following:

- How much of your day is spent on things that don't really matter?
- How can you find happiness through mindfulness, even in the mundane?
- How will you make *this* day better than the one before?

CHAPTER 4. WHAT IS HAPPENING IN THIS MOMENT?

We have only this moment, sparkling like a star in our hand and melting like a snowflake. —Francis Bacon

There is only this moment. The past is a memory, the future a mirage in the distance. This is the waypoint between all that has ever been and all that will ever be, and the medium through which we connect to the beauty, truth, and goodness in ourselves, others, the past, and the future.

Our lives begin and end in a moment. Those between are filled with a vast stream of potential—happiness, sadness, anticipation, exultation, insight, and wonder—all the complementary colors of the spectrum of life. Once we open ourselves to this stream, the atmosphere is charged with everything we need to be complete. But just as the photographer Henri Cartier-Bresson remarked, if we are not in the present, "Oop! The Moment! Once you miss it, it is gone forever."[5]

Think about the undeniable pleasures of life—listening to music, taking in a beautiful view, or sharing a meal with someone we care about. Even approaching these with the sincerest intention of remaining in the present, we often discover our minds drifting.

Why is that?

For example, how long can you continue reading these words without an intruding thought? A few sentences? Several paragraphs? Or if you have the concentration, you might read several pages before your thinking mind disrupts your harmonic mind. You disconnect. And then, for the moment, the cause is lost. Maybe you find yourself looking out the window, idly studying the weather. Your back is aching. You start wondering what's for dinner . . .

It feels as though we're never really *here*; rather, we're always on our way *there*, because the future, we promise, is where we will have time to attend to the moment. Meanwhile, our list of to-dos grows ever longer. Even as we work, we often try to perform ten tasks at once while fantasizing about other things. Then we go home and deliberately self-medicate or fill our time with diversions, denying ourselves the pleasure and joy we long for, irretrievably losing touch with the immediacy of experience. We sense this disconnection from the present most keenly when it affects the people we love. We have our excuses, our reasons, sometimes our little scores to settle; in any case, we learn to listen with one ear, unwilling or afraid to stop and openly connect. Instead, we develop conventions that govern our communication and distance us even further from those we care about. Then one day when we least expect it, they're gone; the opportunity to say what we really wanted to say is lost forever.

To turn things around, we must willingly sacrifice giving in to the distractions of today. The future we want is only an ever-receding mirage until we can be honest enough to recognize when we're wasting time and summon the strength to focus on what we truly desire. Put another way, unless we are *here*, we will never get *there*, and our future is left to the mercy of chance.

For My Self

We do not see things as they are, we see them as we are. —Anaïs
Nin

What do we say *when* we notice we are disconnected? We
say *we haven't heard from someone*; that we have *lost touch*.
Likewise, when we are apprehensive, we say something
doesn't feel right. Or when someone says something inappropriate, we say their comment is *in bad taste*. Our language
mirrors our physical connection to the world.

Our senses were the first tools we used to understand our
surroundings. They provided the assurances and warnings we
used to navigate the blooming, buzzing confusion of a toddler's
world: those hissing, blue flames from the stove will burn us;
that sweet-smelling pie will taste good. Our sensory experiences became perceptions, mental signs suggesting significance
more or less distinct from the sensation itself. Perceptions
form the basis of how we interpret our environment, as well
as of the language we use to express these interpretations.

We know how easily our experiences can be colored when
we feel tired and irritable, edgy and agitated, or peaceful
and at ease. Such feelings powerfully affect our perceptions,
possibly blinding us to a child's timid smile, deafening us to
a friend's subtle plea for help, or energizing the body with
that first pine-scented lungful of mountain air. Our senses
continuously sending and receiving information, our minds
process the raw information into the perceptions that inform our awareness. While much of this is automatic and
unconscious, refocusing attention on pure sensation sharpens these perceptions and ensures they are not distorted
by the preconceptions and fears we project onto the world.

How do we discern truth?

It may come as a surprise, but it is possible to be seemingly "in touch with reality," yet completely at odds with the rest of the world. Every individual interprets the world through a different set of subconscious mental filters formed from their beliefs and experiences. In this sense, then, individual truth is indeed in the eye of the beholder. Real truth, or the whole truth, emerges when we see things as they are, *not* as we have come to expect them to be or as we fear they might be.

To make the best choices in pursuing our life's purpose, we need to calibrate our senses to respond with *curiosity* to whatever we perceive—rather than react, to see things as they *are*, not as an average of past experience or in relation to the scary shadows they cast or even in response to the immediate sensation of pleasure or pain they provide. To investigate the physical environment with the greatest accuracy, it helps to remain relaxed, connected, and alert, reducing the static in our sensory signals. What memory equals the experience offered to us when we are fully present to our senses?

We can begin a journey of sensory rediscovery by asking some simple questions: First, what is my body telling me? What's that smell? What am I touching? What's that taste? What are those sounds in the background? How is my posture—am I tense or relaxed, slouching or upright? So often we find the subtle whispers of our senses drowned out by the incessant chattering of thought. By taking the time to concentrate on pure sensation, we separate ourselves from our thoughts and participate in the now. Only in the present do we find our access point for entering a state of harmonic flow.

How might first impressions influence our awareness?

One measure of awareness is the degree to which we are able to second-guess our first impressions. Everyone knows certain images, colors, and sounds influence perception: The bad guy wears black and scowls. A certain fragrance evokes long-held memories. The sound of a child's crying arouses our concern (or irritation) like nothing else. Most of us are aware of such obvious influences and factor them into our assessment of a situation. But there are so many other more or less subtle ways our perceptions trick us: The coil of a rope looped over a path at night looks like one thing on a suburban sidewalk and quite another in the snake-filled jungles of Brazil. The feel of smooth, warm skin provokes very different reactions when we reach out for our lover or grope for the light switch in a dark, unfamiliar room.

We get a much more accurate impression of the world when we learn to resist our own automatic perceptions. Laying aside the issue of interpretation, ask yourself the much simpler question of how accurate your vision might be. Let's look at color perception. If you are a male of Northern European descent, there is a one-in-twelve chance you have some form of color blindness. The men who are red-green color blind and know it are able to negotiate the world much more effectively than their color-blind brothers who are ignorant of their condition. Their contrasting behavior at stoplights displays the truth of this contention.

Or perhaps your color perception is true, but you are near-sighted, able to see things clearly at close range but not at a distance. Maybe, as a child, you adapted by getting closer to the objects you wanted to see clearly, and by squinting to see things farther away. Your visual world was workable and seemed good enough—until you visited an optometrist. If you are one of the many people to have their vision corrected, you probably recall how shocked you were the first time you put on a pair of glasses and the world snapped into focus. Although the world remained the same, your ability to distinguish shapes improved so much that it looked not just better but qualitatively different.

Now, understanding the shortcomings of your vision, you have become sensitive to the changing nature of your sight. So you routinely have your eyes examined and, whenever necessary, have your prescription revised. Why? Because you want to be able to see things as accurately as possible, and because the clearer your vision, the better able you are to make choices. The farther away you can read the street sign, the more time you have to prepare for the turn you have to make.

If we cultivate the same pragmatic relationship with the whole of our perceptual world as we have with vision, we can correct for unwitting perceptual biases. The reward will be a closer and much more sensitive connection to a world less distorted by preconceptions.

Increasing one's sensory awareness is an acquired skill, something refined with practice. It can be cultivated by repeatedly taking the time to be mindful of what is actually happening throughout the day. The practice need not—indeed should not—be strenuous or stressful; this would only distort the signal and defeat the purpose. Simply increasing our sensitivity to the ways we distort perceptions, we can break the cycle and stop filtering long enough to glimpse the underlying truth. And sometimes, in the quiet clarity of these moments, we slip into the current of harmonic flow.

Listen to every word of the song and get lost in the melody.

Feel the sense of touch flow throughout your body.

Savor all the flavors of a meal.

Reconnect with your senses and unlock a lifetime of suppressed emotions.

For Others

Ye cannot live for yourselves. A thousand fibers connect you with your fellow men, and along those fibers, as along sympathetic threads, run your actions as causes, and return to you as effects. —Henry Melvill

How much richer are our lives by virtue of our connections with others? Sometimes enjoyment is like the sound of a tree falling in the forest when no one is around: if it's not shared, it's partially lost. Some of the simpler and more profoundly enjoyable experiences in life are intrinsically social: a delicious and resplendent meal; a trip to an exotic foreign country; a movie that stirs the soul and expands our awareness of the wonder of life. How much more meaningful, let alone enjoyable, are these kinds of experiences when they are shared with a friend? To be sure, solitude can be pleasant, and some solitary experience is essential for helping us to remain calm and in touch with our innermost feelings. But the vast majority of human beings are primarily social; we simply cannot thrive long outside a nurturing community of like-intentioned people. For most people, good things unshared go to waste.

Indeed, human beings are born with the power to internalize the experiences of others. We learn from one another how to be happy, how to deal with sorrow, and how to recognize the truth about both the genuine nature of our environment and the qualities of positive relationships with others.

How do we increase our awareness of the web of connectivity?

One of the most prominent characteristics of modern life, besides its frenetic pace, is how much we know *about* each other, yet how little we know *of* each other. In the midst of so much connectivity, many of us still feel desperately alone.

Unfortunately, for too many of us, this disconnectedness extends into every aspect of our lives. Although the interpersonal realm consists of a network of connections between people, we remain insensitive to it so long as we are afraid to open ourselves to each other in the present moment. Perhaps, just as we can tune up our bodily senses, we can sharpen the senses of the heart and make real connections to others.

Imagine you are standing face to face with someone: an acquaintance, a friend, or someone you love. Now imagine a thread between your heart and their heart. What would this heart-to-heart connection feel like? How strong would the connection be? And why does the very idea of a heart-to-heart connection between two people in any but the most intimate of relationships seem intimidating, if not outright frightening or even far-fetched?

Our hearts are linked by an invisible, infinite web. Our connections to family members and friends with whom we communicate frequently feel stronger and more resilient. Then, just slightly farther out are connections to those less intimately related, family and friends we see or speak to only occasionally. Extending out a bit farther are our links with the people we meet only in passing. And way out on the interpersonal horizon are the spidery lines connecting the people we meet with their families, friends, and acquaintances. Though they may be impossible to see, there are still more filaments connecting people we know to people they know to people they know. And so on.

Follow the nodes in the thread and ultimately we are somehow connected to every other person in the world. A popular play and movie, Six Degrees of Separation, proposes that any two people on earth can be connected by six or fewer interpersonal relationships. Regardless of the actual dimensions of this interpersonal realm, it is helpful to imagine this web conducting vibrations that ripple back and forth among all the people in our lives.

In the technologically developed world, where social networks easily connect us to the many people we've met over our lives, it is paradoxically easy to lose our sensitivity to these vibrations. In this state of disconnection, we see others as characters in the roles they play in our lives, instead of experiencing them directly as human beings. Is it any wonder we feel alone?

For some of us, it may even be hard to know what human connectivity feels like. Maybe we feel the tug of the web when we speak to our mother or remember what it felt like the last time we spoke to her. Most of us also remember how happy we felt the last time we got a call or a note from a close friend or loved one we hadn't heard from in a long time. At that moment we almost certainly felt a renewed bond of relationship. But this kind of experience has become rare. Why? Perhaps we are so involved with the petty distractions in our own lives that we don't model this behavior ourselves. We forget that these feelings can extend to even the most casual relationships, such as those with our neighbors or co-workers.

How do preconceptions affect those closest to us?

Opportunities for misperception multiply as we move from the sensory to the interpersonal. In the interpersonal realm, we rarely corroborate our assumptions about the motivations of others, sometimes even of those closest to us. Part of the reason we feel so close to the special people in our lives, those we are "close to," whom we feel we "know," is that genuine understanding is so rare.

Everyone evolves, and if you and I are not evolving in the same direction, we are growing apart. Whenever we stray from seeing each other with fresh eyes, we court misunderstanding or worse. How do we know for sure whether a co-worker's brusque reply is motivated by her irritation with our inane conversation or a throbbing headache that makes it painful for her to speak—or whether we are simply projecting insecurity onto ambiguous behavior? For this reason, it is crucial to give others the benefit of the doubt. Whenever motivations are unclear, at least give them a chance to explain what's on their mind.

From the perspective of others, particularly those we are closest to, it is important to remember that we limit or extinguish their potential when we see them through the filter of our expectations or in terms of our own agenda. Imposing our expectations on another is like confining them to one room of a very large house that we share.

For Living Into

When you look into a pool of water, if the water is still, you can see the moon reflected. If the water is agitated, the moon is fragmented and scattered. It is harder to see the moon. Our minds are like that. When our minds are agitated, we cannot see the true world. —John J. Muth

Is it really true that we simply don't have enough time to reach for our own greatness in the present moment? Maybe we could really focus on the moment if only, paradoxically, we had more time. As soon as the rush is over, we tell ourselves, we'll take the time to start pursuing our purpose.

If we assume that the average person sleeps eight hours every night, we are awake sixteen hours a day. If six of those hours are devoted to must-dos that simply cannot be done more quickly, such as commuting, eating, bathing, and so on, the remaining ten hours represent time devoted to the pursuit of our vocation and avocations. Our effectiveness increases ten percent when we are relaxed, connected, and alert. Ten percent of ten hours is an hour. Therefore, simply by being focused, we reclaim an hour of our time. And if we are *really* focused, and increase our efficiency twenty percent, we reclaim two hours of our time.

Perhaps you're wondering whether it is actually possible to give yourself two hours of free time every day just by being focused. You already know it's possible. We all have days when we feel really relaxed, connected, and alert, when we are in flow with our tasks and accomplish everything we plan and more. When we think about it, we probably increase our efficiency by *more* than twenty percent on those days when we feel really sharp and brimming with energy.

Maybe you like juggling many things at once and still doubt the efficacy of focus. If so, take just ten minutes right now, set a timer, and sit silently observing your surroundings. Do this and nothing else, and you will be amazed by the number of sights, smells, and sensations you notice. And the ten minutes? Time that ordinarily flies by slows down. When we are really focused in the present, the time will be there to do what we need to do. All that is needed is to practice clearing your senses, connecting with your heart, and settling into a focus on the things that need to be done today.

Staying focused in a world of constant distraction is, first of all, to empty our mind of anything but the task at hand: to be mindful. When we are fully connected to the object of our awareness, there is no space left for anything else. We simply attend to our work, free from worry, without lamenting the past or fretting about the future. The difference between inspiration and going through the motions is in our attitude toward what we do; the way we relate to our activities determines the speed, quality, and enjoyment of any task.

What other perspectives are available in the moment?

If limited information leads to limited choice, then better choice making means cultivating the habit of examining all the information we can before choosing. For example, imagine you are a juror in a trial, trying to determine whether the accused acted in self-defense. What if you heard the testimony of only the defendant, or a bystander, or one of the police officers who responded to the incident? Each viewed the event from a distinctly different perspective. Even if they intend to be truthful, it's likely they can provide only a more or less one-sided account. Knowing this, how could you pass judgment without first hearing all the witnesses?

Broadening our perspective adds detail to the texture of our experience and increases our awareness of our own and others' biases. It offers us a more objective view of the truth while helping us see how someone else might interpret the same set of facts. And by allowing us to recognize the subtler implications of a situation, a wider perspective primes us to seize opportunities that might otherwise remain hidden. What else is possible?

Chapter 4 Summary: *What Is Happening in This Moment?* invites us to examine the domain of the present

Life occurs in the present. Only in the now can we experience the flow of sensation, emotional connection to others, and the possibilities lurking in every moment. All these are imperceptible to the preoccupied mind. Ignoring the past, the future, and the distractions of modern life, we focus on the moment and create the conditions for living into the flow where we can savor the richness of life.

From the perspective of *self*, simply by paying attention to what your senses are communicating, you increase your awareness of the true nature of *what is*. Your sensory awareness subtly and not so subtly influences your attitude toward your surroundings; therefore, it is vital to calibrate your ability to transmit and receive information. As your awareness increases, you can better gauge the effects of your sensory experience.

- How can your physical senses help you better discern truth?
- How might first impressions influence your awareness?
- How do perceptions influence your physical state?

From the perspective of our relationships with *others*, we can appreciate that human experience exists within a web of emotional connections. In a real sense, we are related to every other living being, all living in the same place and time, sharing a common history. When we open our hearts to each other, we increase our sensitivity to this ever-expanding web. Conversely, when we interpose expectations, assumptions, or agendas between us, we are left feeling detached and alone.

- How much richer is your life by virtue of your connections with others?
- How do you increase your awareness of the web of connectivity?
- How do your preconceptions affect those closest to you?

From the perspective of *living into* this moment, our effectiveness is better measured by the quality of our focus than by the time we spend. We have all experienced the remarkable immersion of complete engagement: the better our focus, the greater our efficiency. Moreover, acute presence increases our awareness of possibilities otherwise hidden when we engage in two or more things at once or are otherwise disengaged.

- How does focus influence your efficiency?
- How does breadth of perspective affect your choices?
- What other perspectives might be available?

CHAPTER 5. HOW DO WE BECOME OUR GREATEST SELVES?

People often say that this or that person has not yet found himself. But the self is not something one finds, it is something one creates. —Thomas Szasz

What separates us from the rest of the animal kingdom? The domain of choice. We enjoy an inheritance of rational, complex, and even abstract thought. Choice is the most precious human legacy and our greatest responsibility; the choices we make impact not only us but the people around us, influencing the present as well as the future. Whatever we choose ripples through the other domains of our lives, carrying us one step closer to greatness or one step further away.

First, let's back up and consider the meaning of greatness. What is greatness? Is it fame, fortune, influence? We see greatness manifested in all walks of life and can easily create a list of unquestionably great people: Julius Caesar, Martin Luther, William Shakespeare, Marie Curie, Walt Disney. Each represents a very different field of endeavor and place in history, yet all are clearly great in their way. While we may debate their relative importance, collectively, we remember them long after their deaths.

The greatness of these individuals, and of all truly great human beings, lies not so much in their specific accomplishments as in the way they lived. People who enrich their environment have one thing in common: they consciously commit the full measure of their talents to serving a need beyond their personal desires. Whatever the goal, choosing to dedicate their lives to something larger than themselves enlarges the scope of their influence.

What lessons can we learn from these individuals? One is that greatness is inherently idiosyncratic. Greatness also presupposes purity of motivation—rather than seeking fame and fortune, doing something for the sake of doing, because we sense our love flowing through it. Greatness demands consciously choosing to be the greatest you in every domain of your life, regardless of circumstances and without attachment to success. And while the seeds of greatness are already in us, they will not germinate on their own. If we nurture and cultivate them continuously, they will flourish; if we do not, like the living things they are, they will wither and die. To a large degree, greatness simply entails choosing each day to live *into our* potential instead of *living within* our perceived limitations.

Finally, there is an irreducible quantum of boldness in great people. The great ones don't wait for tomorrow to demonstrate what they are capable of but devote themselves to giving their best today. They choose thriving over surviving.

How are we to distinguish greatness from mere success? Success is the product of single-minded dedication to individual achievement; greatness requires the pursuit of something more. Consider the following people: Alan Rufus, William de Warenne, Stephen Girard, A.T. Stewart, and Stephen Van Rensselaer. What do these relatively obscure men have in common? They are all on various lists of the twenty richest people in recorded history. By almost any financial measure, all five of these plutocrats were successful.

Each achieved fame and fortune during his lifetime, but none left a legacy beyond their wealth. Perhaps one might even question whether their very prosperity distracted them from pursuing greatness. Even the most creative spirit is often hampered by success.

How many promising careers are sidelined by distractions of fame, fortune, or the endless pursuit of victory at any cost?

Besides luck and shrewdness, the success of many fabulously wealthy men and women is attributable to their devotion to a single domain of their life: advancing their own prosperity, often neglecting the other areas of their life. Greatness, on the other hand, requires a holistic approach.

Anyone can succeed in one domain simply by ignoring everything else. For example, let's say you are a talented guitarist and want to become a virtuoso. Assume that you decide to focus exclusively on playing your guitar while ignoring everything else in your life. You lock yourself in a room and practice all day, every day, and eventually become extraordinarily proficient, perhaps an actual virtuoso. But just what kind of artist will you be? How will you gain exposure to other playing styles that stimulate creative growth? Will you play soulfully or merely know how to hit the right chord at the right time? Moreover, at what expense? How will you fare if you have failed to develop the social skills needed to play with a band or an orchestra? Will you be able to support yourself as an asocial musician with no comprehension of financial necessity? Or will you end up like so many rock stars of our time, great at music and miserable at life?

While greatness is often correlated with success, it doesn't ensure success. In fact, many who choose to live into their greatness never achieve any degree of financial or professional success. While success and fame require others' recognition and are often the product of a given era, greatness is self-defined—only you can know if you are being your greatest self. Those who do aspire to greatness, however, leave a legacy for the future.

The work of Vincent van Gogh illustrates this. Despite devoting his life to painting, he was virtually unacknowledged during his lifetime, and definitely unappreciated. Now heralded as one of the vanguards of expressionism, van Gogh developed a painterly language that enabled artists to express a truth that lay beyond surface appearance. Writing to his brother, Theo, he said, "Real painters do not paint things as they are. . . . They paint them as they themselves *feel* them to be."

For van Gogh, financial success or even recognition was less important than expressing his feelings through his art. Although his name will never appear on any list of wealthy people, his works now command incredible prices in the art market. Indeed, beyond a small circle of artists and dealers, few appreciated his genius until his paintings appeared in a series of retrospective exhibits after his death in 1890. A century later, in 1990, his *Portrait of Dr. Gachet* sold at auction for $82 million, at that time the highest price ever paid for a work of art. Yet during his lifetime, van Gogh sold only one painting, *The Red Vineyard*, for the princely sum of four hundred francs. Whatever the prices of his paintings, the value of van Gogh's work is measurable by its influence on artists across many disciplines, including architecture, literature, theatre, dance, film, and music. One wonders how many creative people are stifled by the mores and tastes of the era they're born in.

Once we understand that greatness is a choice, it is important to learn why we are not paying more attention to the voice of wisdom that shows us the way. Maybe always making the right choices seems too hard. Or maybe we hold back and ignore our better nature because failure is a distinct possibility. Fear of failure can cause even the stoutest heart to hesitate. It is easier and safer to console ourselves with the thought that we "could have been great" if only we had given our best. Regardless, the more we realize what we're capable of, the harder it is to ignore our voice of wisdom.

Our task then is to discover what makes us feel alive and awaken to the visceral realization that life is all too short. If we can do this and not turn away, we trade the chance of success for the choice to be great.

For My Self

As human beings, our greatness lies not so much in being able to remake the world—that is the myth of the atomic age—as in being able to remake ourselves. —Gandhi

Although it is natural to doubt one's potential for greatness, the potential exists within us all. Sometimes it just takes the proper circumstances to bring it forward.

Let's say you have average balance. Would you be willing to walk a ten-foot-long, twelve-inch-wide plank from one end to the other if it were lying on the ground? Of course. Would you lose your balance? Probably not. What if that same plank were laid between the windows of two buildings ten stories off the ground—and you had to cross it during a violent thunderstorm? No one but a professional daredevil would be willing to walk a slick plank that high off the ground, right? However, what if you were in one building and the other was on fire, and someone you loved—your wife or child—was in that burning building? The wind is howling and the rain is falling in sheets, but their only hope is that you will walk across the plank and carry them to safety. The probability of your trying to cross that plank is now closer to 100 percent. The actual physical act remains the same, but your desire to save the person you love outweighs your fear of falling. Context changes everything.

This dire scenario is unlikely for the average person. Yet such urgency is easy to imagine, and we can also be relatively confident of how we would act under various conditions. This simple thought experiment is a compelling demonstration of the potential within each person and shows how courageous people can be when circumstances demand.

Knowing this, what else might we be capable of?

Of course, heroism is only one aspect of human greatness. While it takes a certain courage to become great in any realm, for most people it is more valuable to identify the nature of their potential, regardless of the courage needed to realize it. In what ways might we make our greatest contributions to the world?

We can discern the general sphere of our potential by thinking about those we most admire and analyzing our role models' characteristics. What makes us admire someone and want to emulate them? What we most admire in others often points to the same virtues or talents that already reside within us.

Who are your personal heroes and what do your heroes stand for? What values do they represent? What are the common traits of the people you admire? Are they willing to risk their lives to achieve their goals? Do they work for changes that improve the quality of life for others? Do they expand the limits of human imagination?

Now, reflecting on your own life, consider the ways your behavior exhibits some of the characteristics of your heroes. Think of the high points in your life, the events and moments when you have been the *best you*. As you notice virtues that seem related to what calls you, consider how you might bring these same qualities into the other domains of your life. How would the best you think, speak, and act to address an unmet need? You can be confident you are living into your greatness when you notice three things:

- First, you feel vibrantly alive and free to express your creativity.
- Second, you see how your life's work benefits not only you but others as well.
- Third, over time, you find *more* ways to provide what others want and need.

Until you gain confidence that you are living this way, you have no idea what is at stake, not only in your life but also in the lives of everyone you influence. The momentum of living into your greatest self builds upon the multitude of routine choices you make every day. Each choice brings the opportunity for incremental progress. Listening to your voice of wisdom and living into being your best self, you will find the momentum increasing, creating a subtle bow wave of inspiration in those you affect, one that ripples out beyond them through the choices *they* make.

For Others

Greatness lies, not in being strong, but in the right using of strength; and strength is not used rightly when it serves only to carry a man above his fellows for his own solitary glory. He is the greatest whose strength carries up the most hearts by the attraction of his own. —Henry Ward Beecher

Can you pursue greatness only for yourself? You can't—because that would be a contradiction in terms. People intuitively sense the limitations of someone whose actions appear shallow or self-centered; their very lack of wholeness renders their accomplishments somehow uninspiring. Like the five plutocrats, very talented people who focus their energies on nothing except individual advancement can achieve enormous success, but it is transitory. So long as they care only about themselves, they will always be incomplete.

Great people touch the deepest part of our humanity. The teacher whose lifelong passion is to awaken the minds of her students inspires us, and we call her a *great* teacher. The tireless medical workers who risk their lives to care for the seriously ill humble us, and we call them *great* doctors and nurses. Greatness may be in the service of thousands or just one other person. But greatness always requires the ability and willingness to help others attain wholeness, with no attachment to the prospect of achieving fame, fortune, or influence.

At twenty-two, Julia plays the lead role in the most successful show on Broadway. She has dedicated hundreds of hours to practicing her craft and now, twice a day, she shares her voice with an audience of appreciative listeners. But she wasn't always so well known. Julia grew up in a middle-class suburb of a city that did little to cultivate the arts. At twenty-one, she took a risk and moved to New York, where she competed against the most talented performers for roles. Finally, she was cast in the chorus, and bigger parts followed. Now her name tops the marquee, and her voice fills sold-out theaters each night.

Julia succeeded, but this story isn't about Julia. It's about David, her father, and how he created the possibility of Julia's success.

David grew up an orphan in the care of the Catholic Charities. As a young man, he began following the path to priesthood. A great student of history and religion, David excelled in divinity school. But as he matured, he discovered his passions lay outside the church: he loved a woman and wanted a family. He left the priesthood, married, and matriculated into law school. Fresh out of school and with a child on the way, David took a job as a county parole officer, a low-paying job few people wanted or appreciated. But David liked helping people. He wanted those in the worst circumstances to have the best possible chance of reentering society.

After several years working for the county, David left that post to work for himself. He now had three young children and wanted more flexibility to spend time with his family. He moved into private practice and in short order had a growing practice. Attracted solely by word of mouth, his clients came from all walks of life. Although David's success rate in court was no better or worse than his peers', his clients referred their friends to him because they liked and trusted him. He looked for the best in his clients, guilty or innocent, and did his best to get them out of the justice system and back to productive lives.

By the time he reached his sixties, David was a silver-haired eminence in the courthouse. Although his experience and reputation merited a high fee, he never charged more than his client could afford or what he believed his services were worth. As a result, his family lived well but modestly.

While David's professional life was not extremely lucrative, it allowed him to maximize his time with his family. Almost every day he could be found having lunch with his wife or one of his children. Just like his clients, even when they failed, his children knew he wanted the best for them. This freedom gave them the space to succeed, and succeed they did. They flourished, because David shaped his own life and attitudes in ways that helped his family blossom.

Today, David's children are not only successful—one is a doctor and another a Broadway singer—but happy. While the world might not know who he was, *they* do—because he was there for them every day. While his greatness lay not in pursuing recognition and making lots of money, he was suited for his work. He was adept at seeing the best in people, even when others could not. Rather than judge, he helped. David was a good lawyer, but he was a *great* father.

Every rocket ship needs fuel to launch it to the heights it is intended for. Some people, like Julia, are rockets. Other people, like David, find pleasure and meaning in fueling others' success. Who is to say whose life is greater?

Our wholeness—and therefore our greatness—can be expressed only through offering others our best and without expectation. The most profound joy comes from caring for others unconditionally and bringing out the best in them. The ultimate measure of your worth is not whether *you* are bigger as a result of your actions but whether *others* are bigger as a result of your influence in their lives. The question is, are you willing to live into your greatness—even if it does not entail fame, fortune, and influence?

For Living Into

Between stimulus and response there is a space. In that space is our power to choose our response. In our response lies our growth and our freedom. —Viktor Frankl

The human mind has unlimited potential. Early in life, we learned we have the power to make positive and negative choices with consequences for ourselves as well as others. We can choose to forgive or choose to take revenge, to enjoy another's happiness or to envy them, to blame someone else for our actions or to take responsibility for what we do. We know what we are capable of if we dare embrace it.

Not only can we guide our actions but, because we are aware of cause and effect, we foresee the consequences of our actions, thoughts, and words. We know that sufficient sleep helps us think clearly, that driving fast on an icy road can cause a wreck, and that practicing with focus improves performance. Our voice of wisdom knows which choices lead toward greatness. And like a glimmer of truth in a shuttered mind, it beckons us to wonder, *what keeps me from being the best me?*

Gaining entry to many of the realms of human attainment involves first unraveling a paradox; indeed, paradox is almost a seal of truth. One such paradox is the necessity of choosing a life in which we risk failing, perhaps even spectacularly. Giving our lives over to a commitment that demands complete engagement requires a love of something greater than ourselves. This is not a question of belief—belief gives rise to doubt, only overcome through a leap of faith. Love, though, leaves no gaps, transcending all beliefs.

Doing what you truly love means developing a tolerance for risk, because often, success follows a series of preliminary setbacks. In developing this tolerance, you learn to pick yourself up and try again, benefiting from the learning that comes only from mistakes—part of what Nietzsche meant when he said, "That which does not kill me only makes me stronger."

Consider that while lesser ventures may be worthwhile only if you succeed, a project undertaken for a noble reason is valuable no matter the outcome. Taking calculated risks brings you closer to the creative tension that resonates within the gap and makes you feel alive.

Consciously choosing a purpose larger than yourself frees you from the encumbrance of *wanting* to succeed. Mistakes compel you to close the gap between the status quo and your full potential—and inevitably, we all make mistakes. Fortunately, though, we are self-authoring. By periodically engaging in open inquiry, we can reevaluate the next steps on our paths to greatness. Our choices may seem bewildering.

It may seem that change is destructive, that everything will fall apart when we abandon the certain but unsatisfying past to embrace an uncertain but promising future. The narrative of our old dreams can be reimagined as something that serves us today, a process as gradual as an autumn leaf changing from green to red, or as dramatic as the phoenix emerging from the fire. But the answer exists within us. If we see clearly who we are in the moment, we can measure the gap between reality and potential—who we are and who we are meant to be. The question now becomes, how do we exploit the creative energy resonating within this gap?

- By distinguishing between intent and expectation.
- By setting positive intentions.
- By being our best selves.

Greatness is achieved by focusing thought, word, and deed on intent. Intentions give you direction while keeping open the possibility for something even greater, ignoring external circumstances and approaching the world only as you would make it. Expectations, on the other hand, create limitations by factoring in circumstances you have no control over. Living into your greatness is a function of choosing to be your best self without expectation. By concentrating on being your best, you are assured of enjoying the journey *itself* regardless of outcome. What's more, in doing so you experience the satisfaction of knowing you are making the world a better place.

Within each of us resides the power to achieve greatness. Why not start now?

Chapter 5 Summary: *How Do We Become Our Greatest Selves?* invites us to examine the domain of choice

Greatness is a choice, an act of will. Greatness does not *happen* to us; it is original, idiosyncratic, and attained only by people who willingly offer their talents in the service of something larger than themselves. Great people act with purity of motivation—channeling effort and energy into something they love that others want and need.

Although greatness is often conflated with success, many truly great people are not successful in the sense of becoming rich or famous, and many outwardly successful people never achieve greatness. This is because greatness requires a holistic approach. Being our best selves in all domains of our lives leads to wholeness—and becoming whole is the path to greatness.

From the perspective of *self*, realize that greatness resides within us all, even if living into it takes courage. Caring about something beyond ourselves catalyzes this courage within us. Usually, of course, it's easier to see qualities of greatness in those we admire. But the particular qualities we appreciate in others already exist within us, ready to shine through.

- What would you not do for someone or something you love?
- Why not bring forward that same spirit in everything you do?
- How would your best self respond to the needs of this very moment?

From the perspective of interactions with *others*, understand that the pursuit of greatness benefits the whole. People devoted to living into their greatness consciously seek to improve every aspect of their lives. Moreover, greatness exists on every scale. Some people express theirs through loving one other person with all their heart, while others give their hearts to improve the world.

- How does greatness encompass service to others?
- What greatness can you imagine that doesn't include fame, fortune, and influence?
- How committed are you to pursuing greatness without attachment to success?

Finally, from the perspective of *living into* greatness, remember that as self-aware beings, we have choices. We can foresee the consequences of our thoughts, words, and actions and understand that greatness is a product of our intentions. Moreover, greatness entails personal risk, the actual *commitment* to something greater with a corresponding possibility of failure. Without a willingness to take risks, we miss the opportunity to learn where our greatness lies. Our purpose is not merely to succeed; rather, our purpose is to realize our greatest potential.

- What is the value of setting intentions?
- How do your expectations necessarily limit your potential?
- How is living into greatness a choice?

PART 2: ADVOCACY

Knowing others is intelligence; knowing yourself is true wisdom. Mastering others is strength; mastering yourself is true power. —Lao Tzu

Our questions of inquiry extended, now what?

Let's begin by reflecting on the questions:

Who am I? asks us to embrace our reason for being.

How do I impact others? asks us to look deeply into our relationship with others.

How will I spend this day? asks us to consciously choose the way we spend our time.

What is happening in this moment? challenges us to live life as it happens instead of allowing it to slip away. And,

How do we become our greatest selves? summons from us the courage to *use ourselves up* in fulfilling our potential rather than *be used up* following lesser pursuits.

Together, these simple questions form the basis of our inquiry, connecting us with reality across each of the domains of our life and directing our thinking toward an increasing circle of concern.

As each inquiry opens new space, our immediate instinct may be to fill it with an answer and marshal evidence to support the answer. But trying to find the answer, the *one* answer, can kill the question. Any sweeping generalization merely suggests that we know all there is to know, when we may only have arrived at a narrow stratum of meaning and interpretation within a larger realm of truth.

Our responses are as important as our questions. They delimit our potential—enlarging or reducing what we believe to be possible. If someone asks you, for example, "What color is the sky?" you might automatically reply, "Blue." But what does that tell you? Surprisingly little. Such decisiveness precludes the opportunity to examine the question from a range of different and possibly more satisfying perspectives. Not only is the sky much more than "blue," the word "blue" itself connotes a greater range of nuance than might first be apparent. Instead of trying to find *the* answer, what if you relate to each question in a way that leaves its integrity intact, allowing your responses to evolve over time? Allowing for the possibility that multiple correct responses exist for any question enlarges our perspective, increasing the number of viable options for getting from point A to point B.

Now, it might seem as though the questions *have* no answers, that they are provocative riddles, such as, "What is the sound of one hand clapping?" What this elusiveness really indicates, however, is that each question has many answers. Like the living beings that suggest them, many answers evolve over time—which does not imply that we cannot share insights and wisdom. Rather, it reminds us that as we deepen our understanding of other perspectives and how our own choices influence the environment, we benefit from being alert and adapting to changes as they arise.

This doesn't mean that in our daily lives there is no critical need for immediate solutions to immediate problems. Holding a mushroom, ready to eat it, we might ask, "Is this mushroom poisonous or edible?" seeking only a one-word answer. We have no need to know the mushroom's life history and phylogenesis in the web of life; we merely need to know whether we can safely pop it into our mouth (and whether it will taste good if we do). At the same time, it seems wise to remember that some answers may remain shrouded from our view—perhaps for many years and perhaps forever. Not only is the world stranger than we think, it is stranger than we *can* think.[6] We are blessed if we can live comfortably in relation to life's mysteries, so we don't squander our time in search of one final answer.

In lieu of seeking *the one* answer from an external source, what we can do is commit to a set of internal guiding principles to advocate. Advocacy is often described as a plea to defend or support a cause or policy, and, in the public realm, as a process of influencing policy and resource allocation in a political, economic, or social context. For our purposes, though, *advocacy* is the practice of intentionally actualizing the potential available within each moment. Advocacy is expressed through our commitment to live into the intentions we form in response to questions of inquiry. While inquiry rewards us with insight into what *is*, advocacy points to what *can be*.

Like inquiry, advocacy is a practice.

The first step toward forming an advocacy is to acknowledge a need—one that transcends any unhealthy, immediate desires of our own small self.

The next is to form positive intentions to address the need.

Finally, integrate them into a singular guiding principle.

We all have an innate knowledge of right and wrong; we know intuitively, for example, not to harm or exploit others.

We may think, *be respectful to your elders. Be gentle with children. Be sensitive to others' vulnerabilities.* These amorphous intentions can be integrated into the principle "be kind." Once we declare our commitment to this principle, it begins to shape our thoughts, words, and actions, impelling us to respond to that need with the fullest expression of our being. It is important, though, to understand that no guiding principle is a complete response to an inquiry, any more than a finger pointing at the moon is the moon. Rather, a guiding principle suggests a condition to satisfy when responding to an inquiry. In other words, if we adopt "be kind" as a principle to advocate, our first commitment would be to embody kindness. As a threshold, any response to "How do I impact others?" should satisfy the guiding principle of be kind. Now we can mold our intentions into a practice until what we stand for becomes our natural inclination. How would the best me express kindness?

At an individual level, only you can determine what is most important for you to advocate in your life: Only you know the context in which your intentions arise, how you relate to them, and what legacy you intend to create. And only you know whether the voice of wisdom concurs.

Family, friends, and trusted advisors can offer counsel by asking you questions, reflecting on your responses and, in the process, sometimes pointing to what is already there but just out of sight. Similarly, experts with specialized knowledge abound in every realm from law and medicine to personal finance. These specialists can broaden your awareness of options available to you, but their advice is only as good as their expertise and especially, their knowledge of your circumstances. Most often, their relationships with you are restricted to particular intervals in your life—and how wise would it be to trust someone with incomplete information about you to make long-term decisions affecting your path?

By comparison, our voice of wisdom knows everything about us, even what we sometimes hide from ourselves, the pathetic or shameful things we withhold even when we try to be completely open. Among the voices that crowd our minds, the voice of wisdom is unique in the degree of compassion it extends to us. With full awareness of all our imperfections, failures, and vulnerabilities, the voice of wisdom nevertheless reserves judgment and offers hope. During periods of radical change, it leads us to deeper, more intuitive levels of understanding where we learn to navigate in the dark, seeking only to illuminate the most effective way of living into the possibility of what can be.

We cultivate our voice of wisdom because it teaches us to learn from our mistakes and make better choices. With its help we can root out the destructive habits and emotions that lead to unnecessary suffering. More than any other, this voice has the power to positively transform our lives the more closely we align with its counsel. The voice of wisdom is always there to remind us that we are capable of loving ourselves as we love others, and that we are all ultimately on the same path.

The chapters that follow provide guiding principles to help you form your own responses to the questions. Only by taking time to live with your responses can you determine the wisdom of adopting any principle as your own to advocate. While at times the guiding principles may seem to be at odds with one another, the tension between them increases their collective strength, serving the whole—just as the opposing supports of a bridge increase its integrity. Whether you adopt one or more as your own, the proposed guiding principles offer a frame for contemplating the question as you divine the course of harmonic flow that pulls you forward in each domain of your life.

Remember that the following guiding principles are described in terms of their relationships to body, heart, and mind. Each can be addressed on its own or examined in terms of its various aspects. For example, "Who am I?" can mean any of these:

Who am I in totality?
Who am I to myself (body)?
Who am I to others (heart)?
Who am I to the future, the present, and in a state of choice (mind)?

Recognizing our responsibility—both to our better selves and to those we care about—to act in accord with our voice of wisdom, we resist giving in to lesser impulses that keep us from being our best.

Inquiry, advocacy, and the voice of wisdom together form a *sacred ternary* that constitutes a practice for living into wholeness, helping us to better engage in inquiry and define and refine our guiding principles. These principles *re-mind* us of our sacred vow to live into these intentions. *Am I being responsive and responsible to my voice of wisdom?* If we develop the habit of asking this and live according to the answer, the best "me" gets better every time we ask the question. To the degree your guiding principles underlie your way of being— in other words, to the degree they become instinctual—your thoughts, words, and actions will be consistent with your unique path to health and happiness.

The more steadfastly committed you remain to being your better self, the greater you become.

CHAPTER 6. STAND TALL

Don't ask yourself what the world needs. Ask yourself what makes you come alive. And then go and do that. Because what the world needs is people who are alive. —Howard Thurman

Ernest Shackleton made his first foray into Antarctica in 1901 as Captain Robert Falcon Scott's third officer on the Discovery Expedition. In the expedition's second year, Scott, Shackleton, and a third member of the crew, Edward Wilson, set out again for the South Pole, achieving the record for highest latitude. After setting the record but before completing the expedition, Shackleton was sent home due to illness.

Determined to make his own mark, Shackleton returned to the continent in 1907 as leader of the Nimrod Expedition. His destination—the South Pole. In the course of their "Great Southern Journey," he and three crewmembers trekked hundreds of miles overland toward the geographical South Pole. En route they chronicled such discoveries as the Beardmore Glacier and Mount Erebus, as well as the South Magnetic Pole. Running low on food and buffeted by the cold, the party was forced to turn back less than one hundred miles from their ultimate goal. Even so, they made history. Shackleton and his team had gone farther south than Captain Scott or anyone else before them, planting a flag for England to mark their accomplishment.

King Edward VII celebrated Shackleton's bravery by granting him knighthood. Nevertheless, Shackleton remained restless; Antarctica was calling. But before he could return to the Southern Hemisphere, the Norwegian explorer, Roald Amundsen, took the South Pole in December of 1911. Initially deflated, Shackleton committed himself to an even greater challenge: crossing the Antarctic continent from sea to sea via the pole. With renewed energy and will, he started planning the Imperial Trans-Antarctic Expedition of 1914–17. A newspaper ad of his day attributed to Shackleton reads, "Men wanted for hazardous journey. Low wages, bitter cold, long hours of complete darkness. Safe return doubtful. Honour and recognition in event of success."

In August 1914, Shackleton and his crew left England and set sail for Argentina aboard the *Endurance*. On December 5th, they embarked upon the final stage of their mission: to forge a passage from the Weddell Sea through the ice-filled waters of Antarctica to Vahsel Bay, due south of Australia.

For weeks they guided the ship slowly and steadily through the thickening waters of the Antarctic. Then, on January 24th, the ship halted. The *Endurance* was trapped in pack ice at the foot of a grounded iceberg. Unable to free the ship, Shackleton's crew set up camp on the surrounding floes in hopes the ice would eventually yield. Days turned into weeks, and weeks turned into months. Then it finally happened: in the third week of November, nearly a year after setting off from South Georgia, the ship began to slip under the ice. The vessel now irretrievable, Shackleton gave the final order: abandon ship.

Alone without a means of conveyance, the men were at the mercy of the unpredictable ice. Worse, the floe underneath their camp was beginning to break apart; they would soon be separated from their lifeboats. Having no other option,

Shackleton ordered the men to launch their boats into the freezing waters and set their course to the nearest island, now more than three hundred miles away. Seven grueling days later, Shackleton and his crew landed on Elephant Island, stepping onto solid ground for the first time in almost five hundred days. The barren shoreline was not only inhospitable but far from any shipping routes. If they stayed, they would starve.

Realizing their chances of rescue on such a remote island were nonexistent, Shackleton chose five of his most able-bodied crew to join him on the eight-hundred-nautical-mile open-boat voyage to the nearest inhabited outpost: a whaling station back on South Georgia Island. On April 24th, 1916, the men set out to sea in a twenty-foot lifeboat with little more than a sail, a sextant, and less than a month's worth of food and water. If they failed to reach South Georgia within a month, they would die of starvation and dehydration—if they had not already capsized and drowned in the treacherous South Atlantic.

Against all odds, on May 8th, fifteen days after their departure, Shackleton and the men spotted the cliffs of South Georgia rising in the distance. But before they could reach the coast, nature intervened once more when a storm with hurricane-force winds prevented them from landing, requiring them to spend a harrowing night offshore, at great risk of being dashed against the rocks.

The following day, when the weather passed, they made landfall on the island's southern coast. The whaling station, however, was on the northern coast. Rather than risk putting the small lifeboat back out to sea, Shackleton chose to cross the island on foot, a feat never before attempted. Twelve days later, he tramped into the station to the surprise of whaling crews taking shelter in the port.

Concerned about the safety of the men he had been forced to leave behind, Shackleton immediately set to work organizing their rescue from Elephant Island. But the weather was uncooperative, and the first three attempts were aborted. Undeterred, Shackleton persevered, and on the fourth attempt, he succeeded in reuniting with the rest of his crew on August 30th, 1916. It was the middle of the South Polar winter and four and a half months after setting out for the station. Not a man was lost.

By any measure, Ernest Shackleton was a heroic explorer, a great man who clearly dedicated his life to his dream. Without exception, he acted on his highest intentions, even when he knew his chances of success were vanishingly small. But his purpose wasn't just to reach the South Pole or even to be the first human being to cross the Antarctic continent. Shackleton's purpose was to *explore*; the *expression* of his purpose was to chart the vast, then-unknown continent of Antarctica. In an earlier era, in the time of Christopher Columbus, he might have captained a caravel. And not so many years later, like Neil Armstrong, he might have dreamed of commanding a rocket ship.

If you were able to go back in time and meet Ernest Shackleton, you would not need to ask him his reason for living. His purpose would be evident from his actions. His whole life revolved around planning for, leading, and writing about exploratory expeditions. Through living into his purpose, he harnessed his strengths: leadership, courage, and perseverance. And as a *byproduct* of living this way, he became an iconic personification of the pure explorer.

To be clear, Shackleton's sense of purpose did not eliminate the obstacles he faced. During the expeditions he endured physical distress ranging from frostbite to snow blindness, along with a gradually worsening heart condition exacerbated by a seaman's propensity for drink. At home in England he was revered but had little money to show for his efforts. But the real difficulties Shackleton faced mattered little compared to the misery he felt when confined to one place on land, unable to push beyond the limits of the known.

While few people dream of spending days trekking across miles of desolate tundra, the inspiration for all of us is clear: in dedicating our bodies, hearts, and minds to something greater than ourselves, we become vibrantly alive. In a real sense, our purpose is what we are willing to give our lives for. While every one of us will certainly die, not every one of us is willing to *stand tall* and live.

Root

Effort and courage are not enough without purpose and direction. —John F. Kennedy

Until one *is* (to be), one must continue to ask the question: *Who am I?* The question points toward our innate calling or purpose. Once you recognize your calling and commit to living into it, you connect with the essence of your being and the source of your greatest strength. Think of the people you most admire. There is no need to ask them what they stand for; their intentions are evident in their every action.

To be clear, your purpose is more than your job, your daily responsibilities, or even your goals. Your purpose is the transcendent crystallization of your voice of wisdom, the apotheosis of your best and most authentic self. It is the true godlike expression of your being. When you find it, you know without question that your purpose is the reason you exist.

Even so, it requires courage and honesty to stay the course at moments when understanding what gives life meaning seems beyond one's grasp. This recognition takes time, effort, and perseverance, often through many false starts. It rarely forms like a lightning strike or even overnight. More often one's purpose is gradually revealed through "living into," the way a sculptor carves a statue from a block of granite, or a smith forges a blade from a rod of steel. We might even imagine it growing over time like a tree.

Each of us is born with the greatest potential within us, just as a newly formed seed has the potential to grow into the noblest of trees. As a tree grows from its roots, so our life's work grows from our purpose. In a real sense, growing up is really the process of uncovering, nurturing, and sustaining that purpose. Like all growing things, a purpose emerges when exposed to the right conditions—and though at first it requires that you nurture it, as it matures it begins to sustain you.

The existence of purpose

Let us pause for a moment. Perhaps you believe your life has no particular meaning. While our lives may sometimes seem devoid of any but cautionary meaning, we need not conflate *doubt about meaning* with *meaninglessness*. Just because we are not strangers to defeat does not mean life has no purpose. The philosopher and mathematician Blaise Pascal once considered a similar question concerning the existence of a supreme being.

He asked: Does the possibility of obtaining everlasting salvation (and avoiding eternal damnation) outweigh the cost of a lifetime of earthly submission to "God's" will? According to Pascal, if there is no God, the wise man would still choose to live a righteous life because doing so, he loses nothing when he dies but gains an eternity in heaven if there is. Why not ask ourselves the same sort of question about our purpose? What is the investment of a little time in uncovering our true nature in exchange for the possibility of discovering a deeply satisfying way of life—maybe even an extraordinary life? If we make no effort, our lives are certain to appear meaningless, whether or not our purpose exists. Moreover, an unwillingness to examine our way of being is a willful ignorance that stunts and distorts our relationship with reality.

So how can you uncover your essential nature?

The first step to revealing true purpose requires that you empty your mind of assumptions (yours and others') that keep you from realizing your power and obstruct your growth.

Next, reflect on what you already know. While many personality tests, as well as books and seminars, can illuminate your strengths, weaknesses, and preferences, even without such a test, book, or life coach, you can take inventory of your life. Consider completing the following exercise:

Set aside a time during which you will not be interrupted—thirty to forty-five minutes is sufficient. Take out a few blank sheets of paper and a pen (or start a new document on a computer) and write at the top: *What is my purpose?* Or if it feels more natural, ask, *what is my reason for living?*

Next, read each of the following ten questions slowly and write down the first thing that pops into your mind. A short phrase is as good as a long one. Make sure to write your responses before you have time to analyze them. Don't edit what you write—and be honest; no one else needs to see your work. Make at least a modest investment of effort, and enjoy responding to each of the following questions:

1. What three challenges or hardships have you overcome or are you overcoming? How did you do it, or how are you doing it?
2. What are five values you cherish? (You might find it helpful to contemplate the examples in Appendix 3.)
3. List five of your talents or skills—things you are good at and enjoy doing.
4. List five activities in which you lose track of time (events, hobbies, or projects).
5. List five people who inspire you.
6. If you were to teach one class at your local college, what subject would you teach?
7. If you were starting a new business, what five attributes would you embed in its culture?
8. If you were to volunteer for an organization one day a week, what organization would you choose? What does it stand for?
9. If you had one year left to live and enough money for everything you need, how would you spend the year?
10. If you died tomorrow, what legacy would you like to leave behind? How are you holding yourself back from creating that legacy today?

Please answer these questions as quickly as possible—don't let the pursuit of perfection or comprehensiveness impede your progress. Then reflect on what you have written, noticing the words, phrases, and themes that appear more than once. For example, the words "vision, inspiration, and organization" might point toward a talent for leadership. "Wellness, education, and service" may point toward a career in healthcare. "Learning, truth, and education" may point toward a passion for teaching. Keep digging into your responses carefully to find the roots of a calling.

Now the moment of courage: translate what your voice of intuition whispers to you into an explicit purpose. Start with a fresh sheet of paper or a new page on your screen. Write the following at the top of the page:

What are my greatest talents?

How can I put these talents to use for helping others?

Which of these activities do I enjoy the most?

Next, write a purpose statement for your life—whatever comes to you. It can be as brief as two words—*to teach*—or as long as a few sentences—*I will use my talents of vision, inspiration, and organization to create a business that elevates the lives of others.* Under your first statement, try another, then another until you have written ten, twenty, thirty, fifty, or even one hundred iterations. Eventually, as your statement takes form, your purpose will connect

your greatest talents with
something others want and need
in furtherance of
a purpose that inspires you.

Whatever your calling—explorer, artist, businessperson, scientist, or teacher—if you fully participate in the exercise and suspend belief for a time, you will be surprised and pleased with the results.

Most people produce something they feel connected to within an hour. Sometimes it takes longer, particularly with a cluttered mind or socially conditioned expectations of who you *should* be. Just as a seed transforms when the embryonic form it conceals begins to express its potential, by surrendering who you think you are *supposed* to be, you become what you are *intended* to be.

Don't become discouraged if you find yourself wandering down the wrong path, becoming distracted, or perhaps feeling a resistance to the whole project. You may find yourself thinking *I don't want to deal with this—let's skip the exercise.* Or, *even if I want to do something different, my friends would think I was crazy.* And so on. Ever self-protecting, the ego seeks ways to escape questions whose answers risk provoking real change. All this is normal. Keep going. Be persistent, even if the exercise feels silly or contrived.

And if that moment of recognition does not arrive within a short interval, take a break, walk around, clear your mind, and then come back to your sheet and write down the first thing that surfaces in your mind. Then revise again and again. Eventually, you will see the connection between your greatest talent(s) with something others want and need that you enjoy doing.

Then all at once, *aha!* A truth emerges as if uncovered from a source concealed until now. There on the page staring back at you is a declaration that resonates with your entire being—body, heart, and mind. You know you have uncovered something meaningful when you find yourself drawn forward with urgency and determination.

Now take a moment and imagine how Ernest Shackleton might have completed this exercise. What might he have written? Perhaps something like this: "I vow to someday go to the region of ice and snow—to one of the poles of the earth, the end of the axis upon which this great round ball turns." Which, as it happens, he did. And once he'd made this solemn vow, he didn't let anyone or anything hold him back from declaring his purpose and living into it.

Neither will you.

Rise

When the roots are in deep, then the tree will grow and beautiful flowers will bloom naturally. —Tom Wright

One cannot remain an acorn and still expect to become a mighty tree.

Once you have uncovered your purpose, the challenge lies in liberating it, nurturing it, and trusting that it will thrive—even as your reach extends into unfamiliar territory. Everything in your environment has the potential to advance or retard the growth of purpose. Nourish it by keeping it with you, choosing to live into it, following the light of inspiration moment by moment until you become the best you that you can be. In focusing on moving in the right direction instead of "succeeding," you grow a little each day—irrespective of your surroundings.

Stand tall and rise to fulfill your purpose

The particular environment we are born in—our place, our time—provides the soil we grow in. Look around, though, and you will find a tree can grow almost anywhere—from the banks of a wilderness river to the cracks in an inner-city sidewalk. The natural impulse to grow expresses itself even in the shifting soils of the most hostile environment.

Just as trees grow organically in relation to their environment, our purpose as human beings evolves over time. If you could look inside a tree, you would discover indelible rings hidden within, formed by each season's memories, symbolizing periods of growth, survival, and progress. Only the tree's exterior bears the marks of the many traumas it has faced and survived—the price of living in its place and time. And notice how trees grow. They don't always start growing straight up—they don't necessarily grow perfectly vertically, and sometimes benefit from reinforcement. Like any growing being, saplings may require support until their roots reach a depth capable of bracing their height and nourishing their growth. But the deeper their roots, the higher and straighter they grow and the greater their ability to withstand the inevitable storms. Unlike leaves that come and go, the roots remain for life.

So it is with us. Although everything about us changes— our jobs, our homes, our health, perhaps even our view of the world—there is still something about us that remains constant. Our fundamental intentions become rings in the heartwood of our being. They emanate from our way of being and, like roots, nourish and support us. We know what we stand for, even if we express our intentions differently in different environments. Some things about us can no more change than an oak can assume the form of a willow.

A purpose begins to take hold

Once we know what we stand *for*, a clear dichotomy emerges that illuminates what we must rise up *against*. If you are for health and wellness, you are against indolence and gluttony. If you are for equality and justice, you are opposed to subjugation and cruelty. When you practice living in alignment with your values, others will notice and feel your conviction. What you stand for is more important than money, acceptance, or even personal security.

A purpose that lives through us is one we are willing to make sacrifices for. Sometimes, circumstances demand it. Despite our best intentions, standing up for the truth as we know it sometimes leads to unavoidable conflict. Some circumstances leave us no choice but to confront the negative expressions of the values we hold sacred. If we value equality and justice, for example, we will rise against oppression. Each voice represents another important constituent, sometimes unheard within the collective consciousness—even when that means expressing our objections, dissensions, or demands for what is right. As Martin Luther King said, "In the end, we will remember not the words of our enemies, but the silence of our friends."

When our values irresistibly draw us into conflict, it is better to confront our challengers nobly. We must keep the fundamental causes of the conflict clear, focusing on facts and intentions rather than individuals or ideology. Can we learn something new? Above all, it's helpful to remain centered and resist the temptation to summon anger or fear, instruments of the persecutor and the victim. Rather than using force to resolve a conflict, offer respect. Giving respect, we earn respect. And when the time for conflict has passed, whatever the outcome, acknowledge the other person while reflecting on what you learned. In all situations and in all events, remember who you are and what you stand for.

The self-sustaining purpose

The words *biology* and *biography* share the same Greek root: *bios*, the word for "life." Living is a biological state; living aligned with our true nature forms the expression of our being. Together, our biology and biography inform the narrative of our lives.

As you live into your life's purpose, your survival and growth are influenced by a rushing confluence of social and interpersonal stimuli that are in a constant state of flux. If you are not to be overwhelmed, you must learn to respond intelligently to your environment. As the environment changes, as it inevitably will, your voice of wisdom helps you author the life you desire. You will know you have uncovered your reason for being when you feel it resonating deeply through your body, heart, and mind. Once you take notice, your life circumstances provide opportunities to deploy your strengths in unique ways.

Others may share a similar purpose; however, the particular way you apply your skills and talents renders it unique. You might even think of this process as more of a journey than a search. Along the way, you can use the internal verbalization of your purpose like a mantra, solidifying your resolve by repeating the intention over and over. If, for example, you truly are an explorer, by repeatedly thinking or speaking the words, *my purpose is to explore*, or *I am an explorer*, you will summon a special energy that catalyzes the fire of determination within and opens pathways that lead beyond the mundane. This kind of motivation is available every moment of our lives, in situations of any magnitude. Ernest Shackleton, for example, could always marshal enthusiasm for exploration, whether the object of his exploration was Antarctica or a quaint old Norwegian fishing village he had never visited before.

Like a tree, you are a force of nature living within an eco-system of other more or less conscious organisms. And as an intelligent, self-authoring being, your power, perhaps even your responsibility, is to grow, respond, and adapt in ways that enrich your environment for yourself and others. This is your greater purpose. The intentions that flow from your purpose provide the basis for a higher, uniquely human form of desire and give you the strength to rise. As Henry George suggests, a human purpose fuels a desire that "slumbered in the plant, fitfully stirred in the beast, [and] awakens in the man," giving rise to a "desire higher yet . . . that he may somehow aid in making life better and brighter."

Firmly rooted in your purpose, you gather in the clear sunlight that naturally raises you upward and outward. Be what you love; love what you become.

Reflect

The wisest mind has something yet to learn. —George Santayana

Reflect on the light, the shadows, and the direction of your growth. Until you know who you are with the same certainty you possess that the sun will rise in the morning, keep re-flecting on this question: *Who am I?*

Reflecting on the ten questions listed earlier, we gain a better grasp of who we are and who we are not. We know these answers to be true, because when we are mak-ing the right choices and acting in a way consistent with our purpose, we realize the vitality and contentedness of satisfaction. Living in harmony with our purpose, we feel most whole—body, heart, and mind all united in being—and consequently, happiest. Conversely, when we diverge from wholeness, acting in opposition to our values, we experience fatigue and distress.

When we reflect our intentions and purpose, we improve not only our health but also the health of the environment around us: the people with whom we are in contact, the present within which the future unfolds, and the future embedded in the present. Just as the leaves on a tree reflect some wavelengths of the sun and absorb others, the positive expression of our intentions reflects the spectrum of values we choose. A healthy tree enriches its environment through generating oxygen, giving its leaves to fertilize the soil, and providing shade for so much other life to flourish. A positive expression of an authentic purpose does the same thing. It creates the conditions for positive transformation within a climate of trust, communication, and gratitude coupled with a disposition toward growth.

Seek perspective

The more we align with our values, the closer we are to bringing our whole selves into being. But to determine how well we are aligned, we must objectively assess our thoughts, words, and actions. The emphasis is on *objectivity*, something difficult to attain by ourselves, if at all. To discern truth, we must be willing to solicit feedback from others—family, friends, and people we interact with regularly. Each holds a unique sense of who we are and sees us through their own filter. Nevertheless, a trusted advisor, whether a friend, mentor, or coach, can help us see things in ourselves that we may not be aware of.

If you share your intentions with someone you trust and who cares about you, what might they offer in the way of advice? What inconsistencies would they point out? If you're able to absorb uncomfortable truths about yourself without becoming defensive, to hear the truth even when it hurts, you can learn a lot by asking those close to you to give you unvarnished assessments of how consistent your actions are with your professed values—are you making the continual microadjustments to close the gap between your intentions and your actions? Feedback from those who know you well or who are wise often provokes new questions to engage your voice of wisdom.

Bearing in mind that you are not transparent, you must recognize the futility of relying on any single source of feedback. Even your most intimate friends can see only so much—to a large degree, observing only those dimensions of your life you have explicitly shared with them. You need to be able to interpret the nuances of their responses. No doubt, their growth is as radical and rapid as your own, and their perspectives are shaped by their life experiences. It follows that they have idiosyncratic preferences and prejudices that motivate their response to you. Moreover, those closest to you are often unwilling to say anything that might in any way be considered hurtful; they may even be trying to divine what you want to hear—something expedient or reassuring. Few people have developed the art of constructive criticism. Often, our friends' best role is in allowing us to speak out loud the issues we are facing, or simply in consoling us.

Our present attitude also provides meaningful feedback. Just noticing when you are happy lets you know that, in some way, you are aligned with your true nature. If you're unhappy, it is likely you're either living at odds with your values or in the midst of catastrophe. When you are experiencing re-curring, avoidable crises, consider whether you might be running away from yourself. In the simple act of *stopping* and taking a look around, you may find your path to trans-formation illuminated.

At least once a day, take time to reflect. Ask yourself—Am *I standing tall?* Answer these simple questions:

1. What are my intentions?
2. How closely are my thoughts, words, and actions aligned with my intentions?
3. Am I happy?

The first question grounds you in your purpose, potential, and the commitment to realizing that potential.

The second one invokes your voice of wisdom to help you see yourself more objectively in terms of the degree to which you're living into your purpose. What strengths most need developing? What opportunities are present? Generally, in light of your professed intentions, what should you start do-ing or do more of? And what must you stop or do less of? Your voice of wisdom serves as your guide and companion in responding to these questions.

The third question is a navigational aid that helps you stay on the right path. The more closely you follow your voice of wisdom, the more likely you are to experience ease and contentment. Pervasive anxiety and unhappiness, on the other hand, may be a sign that you are on the wrong path. Perhaps you have mistakenly set out to live like a willow when you are truly an oak—someone who would rather stand firm and give your life for what you believe is an honorable cause than bend with the prevailing winds of a storm.[7]

Mind the gap

As the full expression of you comes into being, you become acutely aware of the ways you are misaligned and in a state of discord. Trying to be someone you are not produces disharmony. If you consistently find yourself acting in ways that are contrary to your avowed intentions, you might need to reexamine your intentions. It is almost inevitable that, at some point in your evolution, you will discover your true purpose is not exactly as you had once imagined it. There is no dishonor in correcting your course, and there is certainly no virtue in willfully living at cross-purposes to your intrinsic nature. Where there is a difference between your intentions and your actual thoughts, words, and actions, there is an innate desire to align them.

As you eliminate the dissonance produced by the gap, you attain a deep level of self-acceptance, quieting the small voice of dissatisfaction that reminds you how unhappy you are trying to be something different. Firmly rooted, you naturally grow into what you are—something more valuable to the greater environment we live in.

In *being* yourself, you *forget* your self, naturally offering up what you are to the world. In the words of St. Francis of Assisi, "It is in giving oneself that one receives; it is in forgetting oneself that one is found."

Chapter 6 Summary: *Stand Tall* advocates that we take a stand for ourselves

The life of Ernest Shackleton exemplifies a life with purpose. Shackleton was born to roam the far ends of the earth, and his greatest strengths—courage, endurance, and leadership—suited him perfectly for exploration. He was the personification of an explorer despite a career littered with what at times seemed to be failure, and his perseverance alone provides us all with inspiration. By his willingness to sacrifice everything for something greater than himself—the quest to chart the unknown, national pride, the lives of the men under his command—Ernest Shackleton found what made him feel alive.

Standing tall, we *root, rise, and reflect.*

Root

- Each of us is born with the greatest potential, just as the noblest tree grows from a newly formed seed.
- Your purpose is the essence of your being and the source of your greatest strength.
- Just as a tree grows, your purpose evolves organically over time in relation to your environment.
- While at first you must nurture your purpose, as it gathers strength, it will begin to support you.
- Even if you doubt its existence, belief in a purpose offers a life filled with meaning.

Rise

- The intentions that flow from your purpose give you the strength to rise.

- Once you know what you stand for, it is clear what you must rise up against and be willing to sacrifice for.
- What you stand for is more important than money, or acceptance, or even security.

Reflect

- At least once a day, ask, what are my intentions? How closely are my thoughts, words, and actions aligned with my intentions? Am I happy?
- The people around you offer valuable feedback. But be careful to interpret their responses; what they can see is limited.
- Notice how you feel: being happy points to an alignment with your true nature.
- Thinking, speaking, or acting contrary to your values diverges from wholeness, inviting discontent.
- Remember to "mind the gap"; learn from mistakes and realign along the way.

CHAPTER 7. BE KIND

Do a deed of simple kindness; though its end you may not see,
it may reach, like widening ripples, down a long eternity. —
Joseph Norris

In 1994, Jeff Bezos founded Amazon.com, Inc., the world's
largest online retailer. Two years earlier, during a period of
rapid adoption of the Internet, the US Supreme Court had
issued an opinion in the case of *Quill Corp. v. North Dakota*
ruling that retailers were not required to collect sales tax
from their out-of-state customers. Bezos foresaw then that
tax-free pricing coupled with a growing acceptance of the
Internet would open a new frontier in business. Leaving his
job at a hedge fund in New York, he packed his car and headed
toward Seattle, writing his business plan along the way. His
vision—to build "the world's largest bookstore."

In 1995, Amazon.com opened on the Internet, offering some 200,000 titles, more books than one could find
in any bookstore. In 1997, the company went public, and
over the course of the next decade, Amazon began offering everything from tubas and golf carts to dishwash-
ers and diapers. In 2010, the year the company's annual
sales exceeded $34 billion, Bezos's alma mater, Princeton
University, asked him to address its graduating seniors
about his achievement.[8]

He started by telling them a story about the summers he spent with his grandparents on their ranch in Texas. He described days spent with his grandfather fixing windmills, vaccinating cattle, and performing other chores, and afternoons with his grandmother, watching soap operas.

One summer when he was about ten years old, he became fascinated by arithmetic. Eager to demonstrate his budding ability to perform basic calculations, he looked for excuses to put his new skill to use through such exercises as measuring gas mileage or calculating the change due at the grocery store. That summer, as they did every few years, Jeff's grandparents took him on a road trip. His grandparents belonged to the Caravan Club, a group of Airstream trailer owners who travel together around the US and Canada.

Rolling down the highway in the back of the car one summer afternoon, with the bright silver camper hitched to the bumper, Bezos looked on as his grandfather drove and his grandmother smoked. The young Bezos disliked the habit and, as the miles passed by, he began to count the number of cigarettes she smoked. Then he multiplied that number by an estimated number of puffs per cigarette. Armed with the statistics from a public service announcement, he poked his head into the front seat between his grandparents and announced to his grandmother, "At two minutes per puff, you've taken nine years off your life!"

Though his calculations may have been accurate, her reaction was unexpected. Instead of applauding his cleverness, perhaps sensing a rebuke, Jeff's grandmother burst into tears. With a sinking feeling in the pit of his stomach, Jeff slumped back into his seat, uncertain of what to do as his grandfather pulled the car off the highway. This is how Bezos describes what happened next:

> [My grandfather] got out of the car and came around and opened my door and waited for me to follow. Was I in trouble? My grandfather was a highly intelligent, quiet man. He had never said a harsh word to me, and maybe this was to be the first time? Or maybe he would ask that I get back in the car and apologize to my grandmother. I had no experience in this realm with my grandparents and no way to gauge what the consequences might be. We stopped beside the trailer. My grandfather looked at me, and after a bit of silence, he gently and calmly said, "Jeff, one day you'll understand that it's harder to be kind than clever."

The lesson that Bezos's grandfather gave him was clear: kindness is a choice. Every interaction with another person is shaped by this choice. If our heart is in the right place, we can say or do almost anything in a positive way. But always be mindful of the ways our own talents seduce us. As Jeff realized, mere intelligence unconditioned by kindness can lead to unconscious arrogance; even truth untempered by kindness can take the form of cruelty. We have a responsibility to reconcile our thoughts, words, and actions with kindness—a virtue equal to all our other talents combined. Thus, our guiding principle is to *be kind*.

All our prophets unite in one message: that kindness multiplies happiness and divides suffering. But what is kindness? It is more than tolerance and keeping the status quo of "do unto others"; kindness is the ingrained intention to *elevate the positive*.

When we recall happy times, we almost always remember occasions shared with others, often when we gave something to someone special, or helped someone we cared about. When we are beneficiaries of good fortune, our first impulse is to call somebody. And when tragedy strikes, we also need the comfort of human contact. We are innately social, compelled to share the events of our lives from the trivial and mundane to the truly extraordinary. Who among us would climb Mount Everest if we were forbidden from sharing our triumph with others?

Kindness demands that we invest care and curiosity in each other. Which is to say, we can't be impersonally kind; we have to be open and vulnerable enough to be able to tailor our kindness to the individual. The closer the relationship, the more important it is to remember to be kind. It is easy to take others for granted or to forget their experiences legitimately differ from ours. And so frequently that it becomes habitual, we fall back on the stereotypes of role: we are parents or children with defined obligations, old friends shaped by ancient history, lovers with conventional expectations. Our most vital relationships don't suffer from a lack of force in our care but the expression of it. She may, for instance, tell him, "I love you," but he believes it only when she holds his hand; he holds her hand, but she longs to hear the words "I love you." People express themselves through a multitude of mediums and idioms.

The misalignment we sometimes experience arises from a difference in the way we communicate. The tools of kindness sculpt, channel, and guide our compassion; we need to be present with those we care about to be able to see them well enough to offer kindness effectively. Otherwise, we run the risk of living in a state of persistent misunderstanding, losing touch with what truly inspires us.

And then there is the question of our vow to stand tall and speak the truth. *Bushido*, the code of the samurai warrior, holds kindness, *jin*, to be the equal of honesty, *makoto*. So how do we reconcile kindness with what we believe to be true?

Kindness helps us to see a positive potential underneath a negative reality. Consider photographs of a dilapidated old house before and after its restoration. Before its restoration, the house might fairly be described as looking awful, even though a discerning eye can see its former and potential beauty. Kindness can and should be informed by a discerning eye, by the ability to see real, potential goodness. Kind words are addressed to another's better self when we need to discuss a negative reality, such as when we perceive someone harming themselves or others.

To activate kindness

- ask open-ended questions and really listen;
- accept others as they are; and
- acknowledge the essence of their humanity.

Ask

The first duty of love is to listen. —Paul Tillich

The first act of kindness is to listen.

To hear is to perceive; to listen is to comprehend. Listening deeply and compassionately creates a pool of shared meaning that encourages real communication. Yet it is not simply a matter of being able to say difficult things in a loving and respectful way; it is equally important to listen lovingly and respectfully to the sometimes difficult things that people say to *you*.

To listen requires *presence*. In a physical sense, presence means facing people, looking them in the eyes, and connecting—that is, tuning out the rest of the world. We show care and strengthen our relationships by establishing an environment where others can speak freely about emotionally charged or controversial topics. The safer the environment, the more likely people are to reveal their truth.

Once you are present, ask open-ended questions: who, what, when, where, and how. Questions such as "Did you have a good day?" suggest an up-or-down qualitative response, such as "good" or "bad," whereas an open-ended question, such as "What kind of day have you had?" allows the emergence of a more expansive response.

With the questions extended, now is the time to listen—really listen to what is said, not what we expect to hear. Keeping silent opens a space for the other to fill. Given the right environment, most people sooner or later reveal what is important in their lives. The challenge is to not cut them off with our own story.

When someone begins to tell us about a place they have visited, our first instinct is often to share our own experiences, either of a similar trip we have taken or of our impressions of the place they've just visited. But doing this, we lose the opportunity to connect and learn something new. More damagingly, we also diminish the importance of our friend's experiences—it's one thing to show empathy and quite another to take over the conversation.

Paying attention to someone is about caring and being careful. Ultimately, caring means to become one with the object of care. Just listening without bringing forward your own story, you begin to imagine what they saw and how they felt—sharing the experience of the storyteller.

Tuning into the speaker, it's equally important to listen for what's unsaid. Just underneath the words, reflected in the speaker's tone or body language or demeanor, is a layer of meaning—often quite distinct from the verbal message— that sensitizes us to the nuances of their perspective. This sensitivity has practical as well as psychological benefits. It serves us well when we solicit input from different people about their attitudes toward possible events that affect them personally, or when we need to base a judgment on what is really important to different people.

Think of how often people have made decisions for us, only to find out that what they chose was something we did not really want. If only they had asked with an intention to understand, we could have expressed our true desires. An open exchange of ideas creates not only the space for healthy challenge and learning but also for partnership.

Whatever the nature of a relationship, the true measure of listening is whether others feel heard.

Accept

Flatter me, and I may not believe you. Criticize me, and I may not like you. Ignore me, and I may not forgive you. Encourage me, and I will not forget you. Love me and I may be forced to love you. —William Arthur Ward

Acceptance promotes kindness and tolerance. To learn to accept others, practice opening your heart and holding them there, rather than in your mind. Notice the feelings that arise when you think of particular people. You may discover your thoughts are often deeply stained with judgment—that feelings associated with some people are tinged with an attractive, positive energy, while others you associate with a dissipation of energy. It's important to be aware of any bias, positive or negative, that prevents you from opening your heart to others.

Forming snap judgments is a survival instinct that has served us well: *These plants are edible; those are poisonous. The pathway by the river is safe; that pathway along the cliff is treacherous.* Our education even rewards this type of reasoning—which is better: x or y? While such reductionist thinking may have ensured our biological survival in almost every way, it leads to gross oversimplification and distorts the truth. For example, how often, if at all, can we be confident in classifying any aspect of our experience as simply good or bad?

Unless we are willing to take in all perspectives—the whole truth—we inevitably separate ourselves from others on the most basic level within a narrow stratum of impermanent and mostly trivial concerns. Life is complex. And for anything to be true, it must be true for everyone; anything less is merely a singular point of view. What we label as good or bad is often merely a preference based on conventions or greater or lesser degrees of acceptance. Ultimately and inevitably, when we apply such crude judgments to any relationship, we dull our desire to learn and limit the inclination to make further distinctions.

While each of us seeks to express our own individuality, we also learned early in life that one of the best ways of ensuring our wellbeing is by forming strong relationships. Our first relationship, the bond between us and our parents, secures our physical survival. Later, we form friendships, which provide social support, and later still we form relationships with our co-workers to ensure financial success. We confirm our standing in these relationships by occasionally testing their boundaries, even as they evolve. Specifically, we sometimes antagonize friends and push away loved ones with the unconscious desire of testing their commitment. The deeper our uneasiness about not being loveable or acceptable, the harder we test. *If I act this way, will I still be accepted?*

Sometimes we resort to marginalizing others to shore up our own confidence. We do this by making artificial distinctions about our relative place within an imaginary hierarchy. But assigning relative values to others reinforces a false belief that we are different, establishing the grounds for a fictional narrative based on fleeting impressions: *that* person must be either smart or lucky, while *those* people lack either the resources or motivation to succeed.

You've undoubtedly observed the following scenario: while you are sitting in a public place with a friend, a strikingly attractive woman strolls by. Your friend gives you a conspiratorial glance. Implicit in the gesture is that the woman is probably shallow or privileged or, being in that exceptional class of beauty, wouldn't deign to speak with the likes of you or me. In either case, by objectifying her, we limit the spectrum of possible interactions, creating a boundary that is, perhaps, a buffer against rejection. But why? Confirming our status as different from hers perpetuates a false notion that her life must be better. What sometimes confounds us is the notion that those we judge—*gasp*—just might share the very same joys and sorrows we do. Moreover, they sense our judgment.

People instinctively understand whether we're coming from a place of love or fear. Others, especially those we care about, are keenly aware of the judgments we impose on them, whether or not we express them out loud. Before judging another, just ask yourself, *are they happy*? If the answer seems to be yes, then, so long as they are not interfering with your own pursuit of happiness, what is there to criticize?

If the answer is no, then how will your criticism bring either of you lasting happiness? More likely than not, people are aware of any shortcomings we point to and would change if they could. Whenever you feel the urge to criticize, remember that we are all doing the best we can. It is from a place of acceptance that we have the most potential to improve.

Practice acceptance

To enter into the spirit of acceptance, start each day afresh, without grievances, with a positive attitude and the understanding that even though the sun reflects differently on different people, we are all fundamentally the same. For so long as we sustain unconditional acceptance of the people in our lives, we avoid creating the artificial boundaries of separation that diminish our lives and the lives of those we encounter.

Within the limits of sanity and propriety, the best way to accept another and their implicit worldview is to employ *understanding without resistance*: suspend the impulse to react in the face of contrary beliefs while examining another person's truth. At least for the duration of a conversation, imagine living in *their* world, focusing on *them* as they tell their story. Imagine as true the premises upon which they have built their beliefs: what are they seeing that you're refusing to see or can't see?

Although it may sound contrived, most of us have practiced this dispassionate neutrality. We've allowed ourselves to enter the fantastic world of children. We've come to appreciate aspects of the crazy logic of our eccentric Uncle Carl, or even begun to get used to the scrambled wisdom of the schizophrenic evangelist on the street corner. Learning to remain open in this way relieves the pressure of trying to impose our own ideals on others. Whenever you find yourself resisting a story, ask yourself, *what keeps me in "my" world?* We all live in the same world, just sometimes we see it differently.

How often do we cut ourselves off from others by automatically dismissing their perspective merely because it's not ours? Extending unconditional agreement, even temporarily, demonstrates a deeper level of courtesy that builds rapport and allows connection. Until we can understand and value others' perspectives, however, we have no way of knowing whether what *we* are advocating is *truly* aligned with the needs of the greater whole. Honesty means admitting how we prefer to see the world, recognizing the partiality and idiosyncrasies of our individual views. In seeking to influence another, we have a responsibility to ensure that our intentions are directed toward the greater good.

Consider Richard. Richard vehemently opposes same-sex marriage. He rails against it at the slightest provocation, invoking religious dogma to justify his scorn. Richard also has a son, Sebastian, who is gay.

Fearing Richard's disapproval, Sebastian conceals his relationships. His family acknowledges that he has "friends," but otherwise denies that he has any romantic interests. Richard even makes jokes and snide comments about gay people in front of his son.

Richard is a perfect test of the value of unconditional agreement, especially for those who consider Richard's views to be bigoted. Anyone who has experienced an argument with someone like Richard, who might cloak his insecurities with religion, knows the futility of a frontal assault; any argument would only harden his stance. So how might we engage Richard, who is unaware that he is making himself and the rest of his family needlessly unhappy?

First listen. Imagine where Richard is coming from. Acknowledge his view, and build rapport by gently asking him questions from the perspective of someone who shares his beliefs. Open the space for Richard to examine his own belief system and, crucially, the effects of his beliefs. If he feels comfortable enough, Richard would have to agree that he has no real reason to resent or fear gay people. But the religious argument might still represent an obstacle to fuller understanding.

We can respect Richard's view on the issue of homosexuality while still expressing our own beliefs. Maybe Richard would be willing to consider the idea of disapproving of this way of living while loving the person, and separate how he feels about an issue from the way he feels about his son. Once Richard opens this door, he might find ways to accept his son. At first, Richard might agree that gay people should have the right to visit their partners in the hospital. Later, he might agree that it is not fair to exclude gay couples from many legal benefits—spousal social security benefits, inheritance rights, perhaps even adoption—solely because of their sexual preferences. Eventually, Richard might finally be able to talk about his relationship with his own son. Building out from the underlying love, and without challenging his core beliefs,

Richard might be able to find ways to bring Sebastian back into his life. A ballgame here, a dinner there . . . maybe, in time, Richard will understand life is too short to waste time fighting and admit Sebastian back into his life.

The degree to which Richard can increase the happiness in his family by modifying his behavior and beliefs depends on the size of his heart and the flexibility of his mind. Some seemingly intolerant parents can find their way to having very close relationships with their children, and even their children's partners or friends, without surrendering their beliefs. Others may choose to remain bitter or estranged to the end. But without creating the space for inquiry through listening without resistance, we make it no easier for Richard to expand his perspective.

Until we *show* acceptance, we will not find ways to bridge the differences that divide us. Harboring reflective anger or ill will only harms us, and anger or animosity have never been relieved by more anger or animosity. We resolve differences not by confronting our adversary but by deeply examining ourselves and our own attitudes. Being the best us gives others the opportunity to be their best as well. And even when substantive differences are not resolved, an attitude of acceptance and the interactions it promotes reduce tensions and antagonisms.

What happens if we maintain acceptance of an adversary? By being willing to learn something new, we offer them the opening to change; instead of focusing on our differences, we focus on our similarities. Even if others prefer not to change, deepening our understanding reduces tension and fear. By doing the right thing—calling upon our better self and seeking common ground through offering acceptance— we provide an opening for others to do the same.

Acknowledge

When a pickpocket meets a saint, all he sees are the saint's pockets. —Sufi proverb

Once we recognize the potential in ourselves, we become sensitive to the glimmerings of this godlike nature in others. In fact, if we believe in a transcendent purpose, an essential element of our existence is to acknowledge the godlike nature in everyone we meet—their unique beauty, truth, and goodness. The first step is recognizing these qualities and acknowledging them, drawing potential outward.

Acknowledgment begins by seeing others from a loving perspective—seeing other people as a family member might see them, noticing what a child or spouse or parent finds endearing or attractive in them. For example, the cleaning lady in the elevator—look to her openly and find something beautiful about her (her hair, her smile, the love she extends to her family through her work).

What we acknowledge is uniqueness rather than perfection. Uniqueness is a gift; it is not, as some incorrectly judge it, a particular set of flaws. Recognizing the godlike nature that flows through others, you may seek further evidence of it in their words and actions. Then, you can relate to them in this way—hold it in your mind, speak to it from your heart, and act as if it is alive within them. People naturally grow toward the light we see them in. We pull them forward through our positive perceptions, along with our words of encouragement and actions toward them. Until they're able to see what we see, continue to hold them in that place.

Our impression of others is a powerful determinant of how they perceive themselves and their possibilities. The moment we alter the way we think, speak, and act toward another, we create the possibility for something different in the future.

True acknowledgment

Acknowledging others also requires letting them know how you feel. You know the value of personalization and specific detail from your own experience. Remember when your mother said something like, "Stop acting that way!" Your response was probably something like, "Huh?" But consider how different your response might have been had your mother said, "I'm so embarrassed by the way you're talking to your aunt. We're going home right now!" Your response to the latter (at least until your teenage years) might have been much more conciliatory, perhaps something along the lines of, "Please, please, I don't want to go home now. I just want to stay and play with my cousins."

A tepid compliment can feel like being damned by faint praise—"You did a good job." Or, "You look pretty tonight." A true acknowledgment is one you own: "Michael, seeing your presentation, I felt proud to be on your team!" or, "Walking into the restaurant tonight, Michelle, I thought, I am so lucky to have such a beautiful wife." For those of us unaccustomed to "feeling" words (mad, glad, sad, and so on), personalization takes practice and courage. But describing what you feel prevents the hearer from being able to deny your words while adding credibility that what you are saying is true.

Begin with a smile

Sometimes, if you don't know what to say or you struggle with the words, it's easier to start with a smile. It's a breathtakingly simple practice. Smiling is a universal acknowledgment of the divine nature in each of us. Not only does a smile send a positive message, it has the reciprocal effect of making us feel better. In smiling, we trigger a sensation of happiness within ourselves as we signal acceptance and acknowledgment to others. And often they smile back. The positive effects radiate throughout our body, from our head to our heart. Smiling, therefore, connects us positively to our physical being. As we feel uplifted, we smile more, sending out more positive waves to propagate and return.

Rephrasing the words of Mahatma Gandhi: When you see god in the next person you meet, it is a waste not to offer a smile.

Chapter 7 Summary: *Be Kind* advocates that we be our best selves to others

How do we impact others? Our guiding principle is *be kind*.

Kindness is the quality of being considerate, humane, and sympathetic to another, and at a deeper level, the desire to acknowledge the godlike nature within them.

Kindness demands that we invest care and curiosity in others and tailor our kindness to them. It is easy to take others for granted or to forget their experience differs legitimately from our own. To make kindness palpable, first step outside any role, offering undivided attention and ignoring expectations.

We become kinder through teaching ourselves to sense the real potential for goodness in others. Learning to discern goodness beneath coarseness or even cruelty, we stand up for truth and gently remind others of their better selves at the same time.

Practice kindness by *asking, accepting,* and *acknowledging*.

Ask

- The first act of kindness is to listen.
- Begin by asking open-ended questions: When? Where? What? How? Why?
- Listen—free from judgment, without interrupting with your own story.
- Attentive silence opens space for real communication.
- The true measure of your ability to listen is whether others feel heard.

Accept

- The best way to show acceptance is to acknowledge someone's beliefs.

- Extending acceptance, even provisionally, dissolves barriers and builds rapport.
- Remember, there is rarely a single point of view; ideas about "good" or "bad" are often merely opinions or preferences.
- Whenever you resist acceptance, remember to ask, *what is keeping me in "my" world anyway?*
- True acceptance originates in the heart, promotes tolerance, and enhances relationships.

Acknowledge

- Belief in a transcendent purpose helps you see the unique beauty, truth, and goodness in each person you meet.
- Having faith in human possibility means affirming it whenever possible.
- Acknowledgment begins in seeing others from a caring perspective—as close family members might.
- Your perception either liberates others from or reinforces their self-limiting beliefs.
- Acknowledgment begins with as little as a smile.

CHAPTER 8. PLAN AHEAD

From intention springs the deed, from the deed springs the habits. From the habits grow the character, from character develops destiny. —Chinese Buddhist text

On April 12, 1961 Yuri Gagarin orbited the earth for 108 minutes before his spacecraft, *Vostok 1*, reentered the atmosphere over his homeland, the Soviet Union. He'd made history, the first man to enter outer space, and his flight was celebrated around the world as a great triumph for mankind. The Soviet leader Nikita Khrushchev declared Gagarin a hero. Meanwhile, political and military leaders in the United States were shocked and embarrassed as a nation grew uneasy. The Soviets were winning the contest for supremacy in space.

The two countries were engaged in a cold war of propaganda campaigns, systematic espionage, and weapons stockpiling that had begun not long after the end of World War II. While an uneasy détente kept either side from confronting the other directly, tensions flared as East and West squared off in military skirmishes throughout Latin America, the Middle East, and Southeast Asia. Closer to home, men on both sides of the Atlantic stood ready in closely guarded bunkers, awaiting a provocation that would set them in motion on a moment's notice. Meanwhile, children performed drills on how to survive the initial wave of a nuclear blast, although anyone of school age already knew the truth: the first to press a red button would destine the launch of nuclear warheads in a response counter-response of mutual annihilation. The rivalry escalated across all fields of competition, from the Olympics to political proselytization in the Third World, reaching its zenith in a winner-take-all space race between the two superpowers.

Six weeks after Gagarin orbited the earth, President John F. Kennedy addressed a special joint session of Congress to announce his support for the National Aeronautics and Space Administration (NASA) and its Apollo program for manned spaceflight: "I believe that this nation should commit itself to achieving the goal, before this decade is out, of landing a man on the moon and returning him safely to the earth." His declaration redefined the ultimate goal of the Space Race with an objective that most in the science community believed impossible. Neither the technology nor the intellectual or financial capital was available to support it.

In the wake of his directive, Kennedy was called on to give a speech at Rice University in Houston. At the time, the Apollo program was fraught with controversy following the Soviet Union's accomplishment, compounded by the mounting costs of funding the program itself. This marked a key moment in the trajectory of the United States' commitment to going to space. On September 12, 1962, Kennedy stood before the gathered crowd to express the reasoning behind his directive to Congress and make a declaration of his own ideals:

> We choose to go to the moon in this decade and do the other things, not because they are easy, but because they are hard, because that goal will serve to organize and measure the best of our energies and skills, because that goal is one that we are willing to accept, one we are unwilling to postpone, and one which we intend to win.

Kennedy believed humanity's exploration of space was inexorable and that the world would be better off with the United States leading the way. The expression of his vision not only reaffirmed his commitment to the space program but shaped policy objectives and budgetary priorities, sparking unprecedented increases in spending on education, research, and scientific advancement.

The year after his "We Choose the Moon" speech moved a nation into action, John Fitzgerald Kennedy was shot dead.

As flags flew at half-mast, the men and women working at NASA pressed onward. In 1968, Apollo 8 launched and became the first manned spacecraft to leave Earth's orbit, circling the moon ten times. Apollo 9 and Apollo 10 followed. Then on July 16th, 1969, nine years after Kennedy's declaration and six years after his death, astronauts Neil Armstrong, Buzz Aldrin, and Michael Collins, the crew of Apollo 11, launched skyward into space toward that bright orb in the evening sky with one aim: to set foot on the moon. Four days later, Armstrong and Aldrin stepped onto the lunar surface as Collins manned the command center in orbit above them. History was forever changed; for the first time, the reach of humankind extended beyond our own world.

To mark their achievement, Armstrong and Aldrin planted an American flag on the moon's surface as a symbol of victory over the Soviets. Although Kennedy did not live to see it, his dream was fully realized four days later when the three astronauts returned safely to earth.

Our third inquiry, "How will I spend this day?" challenges us to envision our future and the way we shape it. Specifically, it confronts us with the implications of structuring a life around a plan—or of allowing life to happen to us.

Humanity's greatest achievements, from building the Giza Pyramids to landing a man on the moon, all have one thing in common: all are products of well-executed plans. Planning touches all aspects of life, from the mundane coordination of our personal schedules to financial arrangements on every scale to the milestones that define the missions of institutions as different as universities and the armed forces. What is true for mankind collectively is also true for individuals: absent a well-conceived plan, we are destined to flounder.

Numerous sayings remind us of the importance of planning: "Begin with the end in mind," or "Failure to plan is planning to fail," or "Plan as if you will live forever, but live as if this is your last day." All these reflect various aspects of the truth that a blueprint for success is consistently setting and achieving goals that build on each other and lead to a desired objective or state. This is what is meant by *planning ahead*.

Even though the chaos that inevitably erupts when we fail to plan is obvious, many (most?) of us find planning our *lives* to be unappealing. Why is this? Why do we so often resist planning for the future? Sometimes we claim we don't have the time or that our vision is not yet clear enough. Both excuses are hollow; "having no time" simply means we don't consider it important enough, and "having no clear vision" simply means we haven't planned. Or maybe there is some notion that having a plan is constraining, requires commitment, or will eliminate the possibility of something extraordinary. But how often does life give us what we want if we don't first envision it?

In our hearts we always know what we desire, at least in broad strokes. But we are nevertheless afraid to embrace the *truth* of what we want and to seek it directly. Does this paralysis arise as a result of the fear of commitment and its close relative, the fear of failure? We cannot be unmoving like a mountain, but we need not be dust in the wind. Which is to say, some of the forces that shape our lives are obviously beyond our control, but the habits we develop have undeniable consequences.

Think of your last weeklong vacation. Consider how you made it happen: first dreaming about the possible places you might go; then selecting the destination, perhaps based on maximizing some enjoyment-to-expense ratio; and finally putting it in motion by making reservations, booking a flight, finding someone to watch Superdog, and so on. At the end of this planning process, as you marked the days on your calendar, there was a real sense the vacation had already begun. In the days and weeks leading up to your departure, you found a simmering pleasure in contemplating the events to come. If you didn't get around to planning your vacation, however, you might have ended up sitting around at home wishing you were somewhere else.

Now compare your vacation planning experiences to your efforts to solidify your career, support your family, or secure your financial independence, concerns that will perhaps affect you as long as you live. How much thought and planning have you devoted to the most important areas of your life? But none of these goals will be realized unless you first connect to whatever is most meaningful to you, and then lay out a sequence of short- and long-term objectives that will bring your vision to life. Everybody knows this. Very few do it.

In taking charge of the direction of your life, one of the first things to consider is how you define the future. Is it ten minutes from now, ten days from now, or ten years from now? Consider that the future is the approaching now shaped by the choices we make today.

The importance of planning is directly proportional to the scale of the dream. While one man pointing skyward in 1961 inspired a voyage to the moon, realizing the dream required the coordinated efforts of thousands of people over many years. Even so, President Kennedy's declaration of his vision and his commitment to the space program were essential. They not only brought his own plans (if not purpose) to life but pointed the way forward for others to lead as well.

Planning not only helps us envision and refine our goals but determines the steps required to reach them. Effective plans clearly and simply describe the results we seek (the what) along with the intentions behind them (the why) together with the methods for achieving those results (the how). Planning helps us make the wisest use of time and resources. In determining a direction for our lives and monitoring our course, we assume responsibility for our own happiness.

To avoid planning is an invitation for unhappiness. In large part, this is because living reactively becomes a cycle repeated over and over. When we resist planning, we neglect the genuine opportunity of embracing our purpose, undermining our capacity to appreciate everything the world offers us. If it is within our power to influence the future, why would we spend one more day in a job that is uninspiring or a relationship that lacks real connection? Absent a plan based on what we stand for and want, we get swept along in cycles of reactivity, preoccupied with what is urgent rather than devoting ourselves to what is important, all the while distracted from any path.

Every day, we contend with a thousand petty distractions that potentially deflect attention from our true objectives. Without a plan, we're vulnerable to being hijacked by trivial, time-consuming activities that displace what is truly important. Accomplishing one task that advances our goals is better than completing twenty that lead to none.

In effect, your plans serve to create a call from the future you desire while marking the path toward your destination. An effective plan braids your intentions with your thoughts, words, and actions. With clear vision, you are better able to avoid crises, as well as overcome your fears of the unknown.

As you connect to your purpose in life (by responding to *who am I?*), it becomes clear that your reason for living is not merely to succeed but to realize your greatest potential, a task that requires dreaming, declaring, and then doing. It begins with dreaming of the future you desire, then declaring it into being—and having once declared your dream, resolving to sustain its growth. Continuing to align your thoughts, words, and actions with your intentions, you begin to create the future today. George Neil reminds us, "It is never too late to be what you might have been."

Dream

How many more times will you watch the full moon rise?[9] — *Paul Bowles*

What was your vision of yesterday? Looking back a year ago, five years ago, or even ten years ago, who did you see yourself being today? What life did you imagine for yourself? The further back you look, the less likely today's reality will match your projection at the time. Indeed, it is often striking to recognize how many aspects of your current life would have seemed improbable, or even impossible, five or ten years ago. Unless your development becomes arrested at some particular stage, you will never cease to evolve.

Reflecting on the past helps us see more clearly into the future. Reflection offers the opportunity to identify patterns, productive and unproductive, and to review the status of our dreams. Are they still really ours? Are they sufficiently farsighted? Have they led to real happiness? When we reflect on our evolution, we should not be surprised to discover that many of yesterday's dreams no longer serve us. They may feel like the clothes we wore ten years ago: too tight here, too loose there, and not at all the style we have come to prefer.

We all find ourselves out of step in this way at some time; sooner or later we have to stop, revisit our dreams and remember what they meant to us. If we remain open to what we discover, we often benefit when we look at our desired future anew. Start once more with a blank canvas. Dream *big*: How would you like to see your life five, ten, or twenty years from now? Envision a world in which we could all be whole and happy. How would such a world look? Allow the mind to wander, ignoring any limitations that present themselves as imaginary obstacles. If you could be granted any wish, what would you wish for?

Dream even *bigger* . . . dare to dream of a future unencumbered by the past. Be willing to conceive of something that might take longer than a lifetime, something greater than you alone can manifest. Write drunk, edit sober. Start by unburdening yourself of the goals of yesterday or the limitations you perceive today. Then, continue to expand the boundaries of your imagination. Suspending disbelief, you're far more likely to be creative in ways that help to bring about what initially seemed impossible. For example:

Developing a vaccine that eradicates unhealthy viruses in humans.

Establishing a foundation that gives millions of dollars to charity every year.

Ensuring that girls in every developing country have equal access to education.

A good vision will memorialize your dreams, but a *great* vision inspires others to act. Such a vision not only galvanizes existing allies but emboldens stakeholders who may have been waiting to show up—stakeholders whose roles support your vision and feel pride in their connection to it. This is true on any scale, whether you're a student seeking to form a group committed to change or a leader asking a nation to launch an endeavor that will take years to accomplish.[10]

Document every idea, even if from your current vantage point it seems impossible. Consider the near and the more distant future and describe your desired attitudes: physical, social, and intellectual.

For example, building upon the vision of ensuring that girls in developing countries have equal access to education, one might expand upon the reasons underlying the need. Education is a critical means of instilling the knowledge, skills, and values that foster the culture of a peaceful and civil society. Eliminating barriers to education invites both girls and boys to participate in a shared language of equality, dignity, and nondiscrimination.

Too often we rush through the step of dreaming. In neglecting this exercise, we deprive ourselves of the chance to enlarge our vision and, as a result, sometimes find ourselves aiming for an easy target—or no real target at all. Begin from the vantage point of the future: If you were standing in the future and looking back, what would you want to see? What are the "trophies" on your wall of accomplishments and the memories in your heart? How will you feel? Who will you love? Where will you work? What places and sensations will you remember?

A well-conceived vision integrates purpose with a plan to achieve it. It is only to be expected that such a future will entail significant challenge and transformation. Be as sure as you can that the purpose and vision you fix on reflects your most authentic desires before you set your course and embark. But do set a course, and be bold. If your vision doesn't scare you a little, maybe it isn't big enough.

However grand the scale of our dreams, as we pass the milestones along the way, we feel the timeframe shrinking and the future coming, and we draw strength from it. An inspiring vision exerts a pull from the future, the way standing at the base of a mountain and looking to the peak draws us upward. From where we stand in the present, we trace our paths, recognizing that each step we take today advances us that much closer to the summit tomorrow.

An effective vision of the future energizes the present by connecting our daily activities to our long-term objectives. Admittedly, this exercise plays out very differently depending on our stage of life. But young or old, we profit from a review of our goals for the future and imagining our world as we would like to see it. What do we need to accomplish to bring our vision to life? How can we prepare for the future we want? Dreaming of a desired future will not necessarily make it so, but *not* dreaming of it will definitely limit the possibilities of what will be.

Declare

Reduce your plan to writing. The moment you complete this, you will have definitely given concrete form to the intangible desire.
—*Napoleon Hill*

Whatever your vision, speak it—or even better, write it—to give it life. Making it explicit and concrete transforms a dream into a real possibility.

A declaration can be as practical as describing what you will do in the next hour or the next week, or as audacious as what you will accomplish over the next ten years or even in a lifetime. If, for example, one aspect of your dream is to become physically fit and healthy, you can focus on what you can do today to advance toward your goal. *Today* I will choose to eat healthy foods. *Today* I will walk for thirty minutes. *Today* I will go to bed early enough to get eight hours of sleep. Setting and achieving measurable daily goals not only builds the confidence that you can achieve the same goal tomorrow but maybe even a greater long-term goal.

Consider the Declaration of Independence: These 1,337 words announced that the thirteen American colonies, then at war with Great Britain, regarded themselves as independent states and no longer part of the British Empire. The Declaration justified the independence of the United States and offered the most potent words in American history:

"We hold these truths to be self-evident . . . that all men are created equal, that they are endowed by their Creator with certain unalienable Rights, that among these are Life, Liberty, and the pursuit of Happiness."

With these words, the United States of America was *declared into being*. And the people who read them were moved to take action. Even after more than two centuries, the words that united the men and women of those thirteen colonies continue to frame the daily lives of the citizens of the United States. Along with the Universal Declaration of Human Rights of 1948, the Declaration of Independence has had a profound impact on the identity and governance of nation states in the modern world.[11]

Declaring your own vision—your own Declaration of Purpose or Declaration of Intentions—gives substance to your purpose. Moreover, if you can summon the courage to share it with others, it will serve as an invitation to potential collaborators to learn how their own skills and abilities might contribute to the possibility of what can be.

Describe the measure of your success

When we put our intentions into words, we objectify them and make them real. Dare to speak them, and the simple act of publicly declaring or privately dedicating ourselves to our guiding principles helps dissolve the limitations imposed by our self-conscious minds. An explicit, outward declaration aligns our choices just as a magnet aligns iron filings.

Be honest about your dedication to each goal. Consciously or unconsciously, we often make commitments that are weak or compete with a stronger, often unspoken desire that give later events the appearance of being accidental. We enter into a project with less than total commitment to shield ourselves from the impact of potential failure—*I never really gave it my all*—and in doing so, sabotage our chances of success. Or we conflate authentic, proactive plans with competing, often reactionary commitments such as, *I will not be my father*—launching ourselves on a trajectory of avoidance rather than aiming for something we truly desire. Years or even decades can be consumed in pursuit of plans that are subverted by insecurities we don't fully recognize. Meanwhile, we continue on a mission toward a barren terrain when the smallest reassurance might have spared us years of devoting our lives to something our hearts know is untrue.

Maintaining a connection to the positive intentions associated with our goals sustains us, and we lose ourselves in the journey, doing what we do for its own sake.

Do

Whatever you can do, or dream you can do, begin it. Boldness has genius, power, and magic in it. —WH Murray, paraphrasing Goethe

Talking and brainstorming, endlessly evaluating every possible contingency, is easy. Without action, though, goals and intentions are nothing more than passing dreams. "Action" describes more than physical movement; yes, action can mean walking, writing, creating, destroying, building, healing, or protecting. But action also involves heart and mind—committing to a clear path toward accomplishing something important. Your vision declared, begin each day by reflecting on your short- and long-term goals, and then commit to action through your words:

Today I will:

1. _____
2. _____
3. _____

This motivational ritual will keep you focused on what you need to accomplish in the day ahead.

Adding a simple preamble or frame will help reinforce the attitudes you wish to embody: "With focus and in furtherance of my intention to learn Italian, this day I will . . . ." Any preamble or frame will do. Tailor it to whatever is important to you, such as "With perseverance and determination to meet my goal of climbing the seven summits, I will..." Threading together all your goals, you might gradually increase your commitments over time. "Body relaxed, heart connected, and mind alert, today I will

1. Learn ten new phrases from my Italian study guide.
2. Run or walk outside for thirty minutes.
3. Start planning the route for our trip."

Maintain the rhythm of action. There are always reasons to give up. Greatness ignores all such reasons. On those days when you are struggling, it is comforting to know that people can endure almost anything one day at a time—even living the day with a broken heart. Remain focused on the *intent* rather than the *outcome*. Some of the most profound transformations in life happen in this way. Consider the people we look to as great leaders whose very struggles made their eventual success so inspirational.

A willingness to step into the unknown is an invaluable skill. How dull it would be if you could predict and control everything. With your sights set on the horizon, you can bravely step forth, then take another step, and another. Lean in and explore, and as you do so, your territory will expand. You will know you are on the right path when you feel yourself being pulled forward by the attraction of the future you envision, coupled with the desire for the horizon to continue receding indefinitely.

In all things we do, it's important to make time to rest. Ritual breaks from *doing* can promote *getting things done*. Our bodies require rest to recover. Our hearts feed on absence to arouse affection. Our brains rely on sleep to rejuvenate and clear out the accumulated debris of the day. And if we don't provide a healthy expression for the need to rest, it will take on a life of its own.

Reclaiming a healthy balance in our way of being sometimes requires us to stop, sit down, and watch the waves roll in. Such periods of quiet reflection are no less important than physical rest and sleep. Taking time to reflect, we are better able to appreciate our accomplishments, the people who have helped us, and the real nature of the purpose we trade our time for. Moreover, when we do return to pursuing our dreams, we return with renewed energy, appreciation, and insight. An unmoored mind often drifts into new insights, sometimes in the shallows and often in the deep.

Chapter 8 Summary: *Plan Ahead* advocates that we be our best selves for the future

Planning is the launching pad for achieving something great. Planning addresses the future, however near or far—the distant now awaiting the choices we make today. While there are always distractions ready to deflect our attention, a well-conceived plan keeps us focused on what is truly important.

An effective plan combines the following elements:

- a vision of the ultimate goal and the reasons you desire it;
- an honest assessment of your capabilities so you can allocate resources;
- measurable milestones to gauge your progress along the way;
- contingency provisions to build in resilience for unexpected changes; and finally,
- elements of appreciation and celebration to make your achievement as much a joy as a success.

A life with no plan is a formula for dissatisfaction; reactivity is a vicious cycle, an endless melodrama of predictable calamities. Planning shepherds us through periods of transformation and channels the energy of change into creativity and innovation. Good plans lead to success; great plans integrate joy into the journey.

Creating a plan can be accomplished in three steps: *dream, declare,* and *do.*

Dream

- Dreaming is a necessary first step; write drunk, edit sober.
- Envision the legacy you want to create.

- Be bold: a great plan has power to unlock unforeseen potential.
- Inspire: an effective vision produces an energizing effect on the present.
- Remember that while no plan is perfect, the act of planning is invaluable.

Declare

- Writing goals makes them real; sharing them publicly acknowledges dedication to something beyond yourself.
- A declaration can be as mundane as a to-do list or as audacious as your life goals.
- An effective plan links intentions to clear, measurable objectives.
- Sharing inspires others to offer their talents in support of a common purpose.
- Be honest about dedication; less than total commitment points to underlying conflict.
- Fear-based goals extinguish potential; translate reactionary or negative goals (the "I will nevers") into affirmative and inspiring goals.
- Finally, if goals are easily within reach, ask whether your sights are set high enough.

Do

- Take care of the present and the future will take care of itself.
- Start now! Without action, goals and objectives are no more than passing dreams.

- Focus on intentions rather than expectations—on the journey, not the destination.
- Don't let reason impede success; greatness sometimes demands being unreasonable.
- Rest and reflect. Rest increases performance; reflection invites gratitude and insight.

CHAPTER 9. LET GO

Q: What is the best time to do each thing?

A: The most important time is now. The present is the only time over which we have power.

—Leo Tolstoy, "The Three Questions"

Not so many years ago a pair of psychologists set out to determine how people respond in the moment.[12] To do this, they recruited students from Princeton's Theological Seminary to take part in a study about religious education and vocations. After completing a questionnaire, each student was instructed to give a brief talk in a nearby room on one of two topics: a passage from the Bible or what it was like to work in the service of God.

The route to the room where they were to give their talks passed through several doors. In one doorway, the psychologists stationed an actor. The man lay doubled over, eyes closed, and in apparent physical distress. The question the experimenters posed was this: Would the students stop to help the man? To add a twist, the psychologists gave each seminary student one of the following three messages: (1) "It'll be a few minutes before they're ready for you, but you might as well head on over." (2) "The assistant is ready for you, so please go right over." (3) "Oh, you're late. They were expecting you a few minutes ago. We'd better get moving." Then, one by one, the seminary students were sent on their way to give their talks.

How did the seminary students respond? On average, only forty percent stopped and offered to aid the distressed man in the doorway. And those who'd been told they were late? Only one in ten stopped. Many stepped over the man, even though he obviously needed their assistance. It is worth noting that half of those seminary students, including the ones who stepped over the injured man, were told they were giving a talk on a parable from the Bible about a passerby who stops to help someone who is injured and in need. The talk was entitled "The Good Samaritan."[13]

Clearly, the seminary students recognized what was happening in the moment, but more than half ignored what the moment called for: helping a man in distress. Rather than stop, however, they chose to be on time for a meeting—anxious to avoid being drawn into a sea of uncertainty, they remained rigidly on course.

Our fourth question, "What is happening in this moment?" evokes the domain of the present. We simultaneously *experience* the moment and *co-create our experience* of it through our thoughts, words, and actions.[14] In the present, we can choose where and how to direct our attention: toward ourselves, toward others, or toward the future. Maybe all three. But always, almost as a reflection of our attention, comes the question, "What is this moment calling for?" In other words, where is the greatest need? What best serves the whole?

Plan ahead, our previous guiding principle, points toward a destination and gives us direction. It also liberates us from uncertainty—where? how? what?—so we can focus on what is immediately before us: this moment. Our minds unburdened, we can take advantage of a wider perspective in making our choices while still savoring the experience of each step along the way. Having and following a plan liberates our attention, allowing us to live into our fourth guiding principle: *let go*. Only through letting go can we effectively hear and respond to what is called for in the moment.

The most successful leaders in business, sports, and politics possess a combination of professional will coupled with personal humility. Undistracted by uncertainty and self-consciousness, they are nimble, capable of striving toward their objectives, even as they remain responsive to the moment. They can see where their attention is needed and respond quickly and intuitively in ways that advance their intentions and values as unique human beings.

Your purpose reveals itself at the intersection of your vision of the future and your concentration on the present. A clear vision allows you to focus on what is immediately before you: the next step in your plan, the person you're talking to. If you cannot free yourself from distractions that fragment your awareness, you risk being only half effective, half connected—stumbling through life and falling behind, out of rhythm with the beat of the music.

By letting go, you reconnect to your *whole intelligence*—the complementary interaction of sensory, emotional, and cognitive awareness. Each mode of awareness enriches the detail and depth of your understanding of the present moment. Guided by whole intelligence, you make better choices.

Once letting go becomes an unconscious way of being, you can live in the harmonic flow of the present. When circumstances call for concentration, you bring concentration to bear with your whole being. When life grants you a joyous occasion, you revel in the celebration. When you are afflicted by injury and loss, you embrace grief head on, learn whatever lesson it has to offer, and hold its hand until it passes on. Otherwise, irresolution seeps into other parts of your life.

Our lives are shaped less by what happens to us and more by how we relate to what happens. Letting go allows us to accept what is and what isn't and live with things just as they are. Letting go offers freedom, releasing us from delusion, greed, and fear, and its outward expression, anger. Freedom from the double-edged sword of judgment, from wanting things to be different from the way they are, and from the toxic belief that things are intrinsically good or bad. Once you truly let go, your whole being instinctively relaxes, restoring a natural rhythm, giving way to a certain grace in everything you do.

The present is our natural sanctuary, and in the present, the natural abodes of posture, presence, and perspective imbue the body, heart, and mind with a feeling of wellbeing.

Posture

When you stand with your two feet on the ground, you will always keep your balance. —Tao Te Ching

Awareness starts with paying attention to the posture and attitude of our bodies. Through its senses, our body served as our original interface to the world and truth. As we acquired language, however, we began to lose touch with the wisdom of our senses. As our world expands, we begin to rely on words to interpret ever-greater amounts of new information, but the very artificiality of language limits our capacity to investigate the true nature of things.

So how do we reawaken our body's intelligence? We stop, survey, and process the signals.

Reconnect to your senses

Stop and take a moment to try the following experiment. As you read or listen to each of the sentences that follow, ask yourself, *what is my body sensing?*

Start with sight. Look—just look around. What do you see directly in front of you, and now farther away? What about above and below the horizon? Now turn and look behind you. Orient yourself in relation to your surroundings. How has your visual environment changed and expanded?

Now close your eyes and listen. What do you hear? Do you hear people talking and laughing in your immediate vicinity, the hum of an air conditioner or heating system? How about when you concentrate on things farther away, outside the room you're in? If you're in the city, perhaps you hear the whoosh of traffic, the distant wail of a siren, or the drone of a lawn mower. Listen more attentively still. Underneath everything else are the subtle sounds of birds, or insects, or the wind—the voices of the natural world. Listen to how sounds emanate from a distance, coming toward you, then receding.

Now concentrate on your sense of touch. Feel the temperature of the air, the weight of your body pressing against the seat of your chair, the texture of the fibers of your clothes on your skin. Reach out with your hands and touch everything within your reach. Glide your hand across the full length of each surface. Measure the weight of each object. Try not to name the things you touch; just stay present to the sensations traveling through your skin.

Now turn your attention to your sense of smell. Take command of your breathing momentarily and inhale deeply. Then again at least once more. Release and notice the ebb and flow of breath. Feel the air flow through your nostrils. Now focus on anything that you can smell. As you take a few additional breaths, consider closing your eyes to enhance the experience.

Now taste. Locate a bit of something to eat, a bit of chocolate or a piece of fruit, or maybe something to drink, such as a glass of juice or wine. (If you are up for a challenge, try a glass of water.) Whatever you select, hold it near and study it as you would a valuable artwork in a museum. Then take a bite or sip and count to ten slowly before swallowing. Notice each flavor. Most things we eat and drink have more flavors than we can name, even with a dictionary at hand.

Take a few minutes each day to practice reacquainting yourself with all your senses. Notice the sounds you encounter, feel the surfaces you touch, and take interest in the food you eat. Taste the orange juice for the first time, each time.

The senses are a sacred gateway to truth, but the sensorium requires continuous rejuvenation to accurately interpret the sensations we encounter. On its own, the mind substitutes habit and memory for direct experience, and, as it does so, we come to take the phenomenal world for granted, eventually becoming desensitized and drained of vitality. Periodically surveying our senses reconnects us to physical reality and to the energy passing through our bodies to our mind.

Release unhealthy tension

As you develop the habit of evaluating the state of your body, you might discover that you are piloting a vessel in distress. Specifically, you might be surprised by the unhealthy tension you discover in your body. Perhaps you hold stress high up in your shoulders, a tension you compensate for by slouching; perhaps you feel stress as painful knots in the muscles of your face, neck, or even your stomach. Each area of unhealthy tension distorts your perception the way a kink in a water hose or spot of corrosion on an electrical connection disrupts the flow. That one kink or corroded spot affects your entire body and colors everything you experience.

Although the fight-or-flight stress response evolved to protect us from mortal danger, it does us more harm than good today. It kicks in as violently now, when we face the prospect of public speaking, as it did when our ancestors heard a rustling sound in the bush after dark. Are we sensing an opportunity or threat? A friend walking into camp or a hungry saber-toothed tiger stalking its prey? The natural instinct to survive sounds the alarm and readies our body to respond to a potential threat. Muscles tensed, heart pounding, our mind closes down, unable to consider any options but running away or confronting the attacker. This is unfortunate, because most of the things that trigger stress and fear in the modern world pose much less of a threat to life and limb than the responses they trigger.

For most, the tension is unrelated to any physical threat. We have food. We have shelter. We live in relative safety. Outside a war zone, the stress response in modern man is a behavioral artifact that has been implicated as a major risk factor for health problems, ranging from cancer to heart disease. Stress also makes us feel miserable. The mind, however, can play tricks on the body. Herein lies the problem: our bodies don't distinguish a perceived threat (e.g., social or relational difficulty) from a legitimate physical threat.

Imagine for a moment that your job requires you to give a presentation to a large, influential group. The presentation is tomorrow. The night before, you can't avoid picturing yourself standing before a sea of expectant faces, every one staring at you with anticipation. Your boss has already told you how important it is to get a favorable response; *you'd better be great*. In your fantasy, you hear your name announced and your palms begin to sweat, your heart pounds, and your thoughts explode into useless, random shards. You feel panic rising and suddenly realize that your mouth is so dry, even in *anticipation*, that you might not be able to speak without your voice quaking. Imagining the first moments on that stage, you probably do not feel much more fear than if you were standing on the flat, open grasslands of the Serengeti being stared down by a hungry saber-toothed tiger.

What you face in this scenario is not a life or death threat. Nor is it even actually happening; you're torturing yourself with what *might* happen tomorrow. How strange. What is even stranger is that we invite this tension into our lives. We watch scary movies, ride roller coasters, and parachute out of airplanes. We may even semiconsciously invite tension by procrastinating on deadlines or committing to insane schedules that leave no time for any contingency. For some, the "rush" of working on the edge enhances performance. Up to a point, anxiety and tension sharpen focus. But this is a game you can't easily control, and, inexorably, one slips over the edge into a stomach-churning, debilitating syndrome of chronic stress. Urgency colors everything, stifling gentler impulses and exaggerating combativeness. Given enough time—and there is always enough—the mind affects the body. Stomachaches, headaches, involuntary tooth grinding, inappropriate and unintended harsh remarks, remorse, guilt, and one (thousand?) too many drinks. Chronic stress depletes our vital force and risks stretching our wellbeing beyond the ability to recover.

Relieve stress through mindfulness

So how do we eliminate or at least minimize this stress? Start by being mindful—specifically, by feeling *where* stress grips you. Your stomach? Your chest? Your neck and face? To release it, focus on releasing these muscles. An easy practice is to "breathe into them." Take a deep breath in filling the space around the muscle to support it, then hold your breath momentarily and concentrate on the area of stress. Now, slowly exhale and imagine the tension flowing out with the breath.

Next consider what activities, people, or thoughts induce this tension. Are you anxious about health, a relationship, or work? Then, crucially, consider whether the problem is inconvenient, debilitating, or poses a threat of physical harm. Is it likely or is it certain? Temporary or permanent?

Unless it is a legitimate threat—a saber-toothed tiger in the dark—it often helps to consider how you would look back on the event in the future. A day later, a year, or ten years from now, what will it matter how your presentation was received? Recalling something that stressed us a year ago is like watching a scary movie for the second or third time: knowing the hero will prevail, we are relieved of the stress and can therefore relax and be present to the whole experience and possibly enjoy the show. By imagining the events that cause us stress today with the same objectivity, we can see through them. Objectivity enlarges our perspective.

Look around—there *is* no saber-toothed tiger stalking you—they are long extinct. Unless you are facing an immediate physical challenge, you are better off letting it go. Just breathe; invite the equanimity that resides on the other side of letting go. With practice, chronic tension will become extinct too.

Recalibrate

The mind-body connection works both ways. Just as our thoughts influence our physical state, so our physical state can influence our perception. Even someone who is color blind can learn to differentiate subtle hues. Thus, as we tune in to our body, it is important to periodically evaluate how acutely we are processing the information we're receiving.

The practices of anthropological research provide insight into how we process sensory information. Anthropologists study groups of people, often by going into a community and living among the "subjects" of their research, recording observations each day. How, one might wonder, do anthropologists monitor their own level of objectivity while they're immersed in an alien culture? They do so by keeping two journals, one to record their observations and one to record how they *feel* at the time they make their observations. Later, they compare the journals to gauge the degree to which their own physical condition and/or emotional state might color their observations. They might, for instance, notice that their observations tend to be skewed negatively when they feel bad:

Moving the campsite up and down the mountains is not only pointless but exhausting.

The hunting party failed again, and the tribe is now forced to eat insects to make up for the lack of protein; I would rather starve.

Conversely, on days when they feel especially vigorous, they might see things in a more positive light:

After six weeks of tramping up and down steep jungle hills, I feel fitter than I have in years.

Once you get past the idea that you're eating a fried grasshopper, it's actually a tasty, crunchy snack.

Like anthropologists, we need to always be aware of how our physical state affects our own observations. When we're happy, we find happiness everywhere; when we're sad, we find sadness everywhere. We can't maximize our objectivity and avoid unnecessary stress unless we learn to calibrate the effect of our physical and emotional state on our response to a given object, person, or situation.

An easy practice to get started on the right foot each day is to start noticing your posture and, in particular, your connection to the earth while walking, sitting, or standing. Focus inward, and become aware of how well balanced and connected to the earth you are in each moment.

If you have ever taken a martial arts or dance class, you probably remember having to relearn how to stand. The instructor began by showing you how unstable your stance was: most of your weight was on one leg, your knees were locked, and your feet were too close together. The instructor then made you plant your feet firmly on the ground, slightly apart, and distribute your weight evenly with your chest lifted upward. Soon you began to feel rooted to the earth, absorbing strength from being connected to its mass. Moreover, with your balance realigned, you became aware of an astonishing calm that prepared you perfectly for physical combat or executing a flowing dance move.

Presence

Voici mon secret. Il est très simple: on ne voit bien qu'avec le cœur. L'essentiel est invisible pour les yeux.[15] —Antoine de Saint-Exupéry

Who doesn't like pizza? Made with whole-grain flour, fresh vegetables, cheese and meat toppings, it can be a nearly perfect food. Take a moment to think about your favorite pizza. Maybe it's a pizza Margherita with a thin crust drizzled in butter, browned and crisped on the edge, covered in a rich sauce of sweet, ripe plum tomatoes. Italian mozzarella cheese is melted in clots over the top, and then there is the fresh basil.

Now imagine that tonight you order a large pizza Margherita and have it delivered to your home. The delivery person knocks on your door, and the smell of pizza rolls in before the door is completely open. You pay for the pizza, close the door, and head for the kitchen. But after the first bites of the first piece, your focus drifts to thoughts of the day, the news, or someone speaking in the background. You become so distracted that, when you look once more into the box, you're astonished to discover that only one or two pieces are left. You're puzzled. How did that happen? You want to experience eating the pizza, but it is all gone and you don't really remember eating it. Then you focus on that last slice, wishing you had more.

Too many of the things we do are like this. Overcommitted, we disconnect ourselves from what is happening in the moment. Worried that we may miss something, we attempt to focus on everything and end up feeling angry, frustrated, or confused.

This happens throughout our daily lives. In the midst of an important daylong project, we find ourselves distracted by a cloud of irrelevant thoughts, and the hours slip past. Startled to find the workday nearly over, we push ourselves to concentrate and hurry, but we're running out of time. We long for extra time—another hour, even an extra few minutes. Frustration rising, we fall further behind as we become more tense and less able to concentrate. So we fumble through the remaining tasks, knowing our work is less than our best effort, or we surrender to failure and leave the project incomplete.

What is the solution? In a word: *presence*.

There may be hundreds of things you need to do, but you can only do one at a time. Which comes first? Start with the task most aligned with your intentions, vision, or plan. Then, in descending order of importance, address each one.

The best way to savor the whole pizza is one bite at a time.

Let go of your "self" to be you

The critical ingredient for presence is just being yourself. Ignore the inner critic. Forget about how others might see you. When you allow yourself to *be* yourself, you stop being self-conscious. Forgetting the self is the gateway to immersion in the harmonic flow.

Remember that little boy or little girl you once were, the one who ran around in circles singing or dancing with all their heart, lost in the joy of the moment? Or more recently, the adult you who sings in the shower and dances across the kitchen when no one else is around? The real you. The real me. We still hear the music and want to sing. We still feel the rhythm of life flowing through us and want to dance.

So where is that voice, that freedom of spirit? Why do we become inhibited and self-conscious?

Our greatest fear is not a scary movie, a speeding roller coaster, or jumping out of a plane. Our greatest fear is to be our true selves, exposed to ridicule and rejection.

To insulate ourselves from such threats, we construct a thick tissue of identity around us. We drape ourselves with possessions, roles, and work, gradually and unwittingly sealing ourselves off inside the comfortable and the known. Separated from new experiences and others, we confine ourselves to a secure enclosure of our own invention. And slowly we become afraid. We're afraid to take risks, be silly, or make mistakes. We no longer sing or dance. So we hide our vulnerabilities, exposing nothing to attack.

Of course this safety comes at a steep price. So long as we remain withdrawn, we're like acorns unable to grow. The longer we refuse to emerge from our shells, the more troubled we are by the emptiness at the core of our lives. A conflict develops between heart and mind, our hearts longing for us to express our true selves, our heads holding us back. [16]

Trapped by the idea of who we are, we no longer remember who we might be. We trade our dreams for lives of habit and routine, and sabotage our opportunities to escape as we cling to possessions that have no meaning, relationships that hold us back, or work that no longer inspires us. Forgotten by our hearts (and minds) is that our greatest strength lies in our willingness to be vulnerable. Only in vulnerability are we free.

Only by exposing our most delicate and deeply concealed roots will we find the confidence and strength to live into our dreams.

We have all witnessed a friend involved in a relationship with someone whose aspirations are clearly in conflict with their own. We might even have risked suggesting they consider ending the relationship to find someone with whom they might create a more fulfilling one. Has this ever worked? Just as we do under similar circumstances, they usually ignore advice, becoming unhappier over time until their misery grows so unbearable that the relationship dies of its own accord.

But life need not be this way; we don't have to suffer before we make a major change. In each moment we are willing to abandon the safety of the known, we become who we are—cutting the cords of the ties that bind us to our constructed (artificial) identities. Such courage transforms lives. Moreover, when we dare to express ourselves authentically, we dissolve the dissonance between who we are and what we project to the world. This internal consistency reduces the conflicts we encounter, because others instinctively trust us when we appear trustworthy, when our thoughts, words, and actions are aligned. Our trustworthiness and compassion emboldens them to respond in kind.

Let go to connect

The presence of others in our lives is a gift. They help us see ourselves as we are, connect us to a larger community, and remind us that our own thoughts are neither objective nor reality.

A precondition for being present for others is to learn and remember their names. We distance ourselves from people the instant we forget their names or try to finesse our way

THE POWER OF 10

through a conversation by using a lot of impersonal "yous" instead of the actual name. Why then do we forget something so basic as a person's name?

The truth is, we have trouble remembering people's names because we don't really *connect* to them when we meet them. We don't take them into our hearts. We meet someone in a group—maybe a business meeting or a party—and even before the conversation ends we've forgotten his name. We're usually more concerned about being seen favorably than really getting to know the person before us, so instead of remembering something essential about that guy at the meeting, we end up remembering how he seemed to perceive us.

People use all kinds of tricks to overcome name amnesia. One of the most popular is the "salesman's technique." You say the person's name upon introduction and then you repeat it out loud several times during the ensuing conversation: "Christian, it is so nice to meet you. So, Christian, where are you from? Oh really? What a lucky guy, growing up near the coast. Do you go back often, Christian?"

It sounds forced and unnatural, because it *is* forced and unnatural. So, instead, you play silent salesman and repeat his name over and over in your mind: *His name is Christian. Christian. Christian.* Maybe the conversation sounds better, but your eyes are glazed over while you're focused on memorizing his name rather than following what he is saying. Even the most sophisticated mental techniques rely on transferring the person's name from your short-term memory into long-term memory. But in most instances, before the party or maybe even the conversation is over, you are on to the next thought—the cache emptied and exchanged, the amnesia sets in. A few days, weeks, or months pass and you meet the person again. The face is familiar, but you struggle to remember the name. *Your face looks familiar . . . but didn't you have a mustache?*

Connecting to others requires both a fearless confidence to be yourself and a willingness to invest in others, connecting with the best in them. It requires seeing others as more than the personification of a role but as potential friends with the same struggles and challenges we face.

Some people are particularly talented at making such connections. The best business and political leaders provide excellent examples of the art of making a personal connection. They can be seamlessly and unselfconsciously "heartfelt," making everyone they meet feel as though they're the only other person in the room. They remember people as part of a network of mutual connections and usually connect their name to something unique about the person, usually one of their greatest strengths. They exude a certainty and confidence that allows them to recognize that every person they meet is important. Often, they greet people with a hug instead of a handshake or nod, and speak with almost theatrical expressiveness, sometimes touching hand to chest as they talk or listen.

So how does someone who is thought-centered, with—as the French might say—*la tête dans les nuages* (their head in the clouds) get in touch with their heart? Try this:

- Place your nondominant hand on your chest over your heart and hold it there. Press your palm into your sternum and stretch your fingers firmly over your chest.
- Now just breathe. Feel the warmth of your body. Notice your heartbeat. Feel the rise and fall of your chest,

the tension in your body release. As you breathe, you might even make a sound: hum, and feel the vibration.

- Close your eyes and consider someone who brings comfort into your life, someone you love—maybe a family member, a friend, even a pet. Or think of something that brings you peace—walking on the beach, witnessing a sunset, or gazing at the moon. Focus on the feeling in your chest, your slowed breathing, and the sensation of gentle relaxation and openness.

As you slowly inhale and exhale, catalogue that feeling in your chest: this is your heart space. Remember this feeling.

If you have done this exercise conscientiously, employ the memory of it the next time you meet someone. Specifically, when you meet someone whose name you want to remember, face them and let everything else in your surroundings fall away, especially thoughts about yourself. Imagine you are meeting a lifelong friend or a loved one who has been away too long. As you focus on the person, take a breath into your heart space. As you breathe out, introduce yourself with a sincere and accepting smile. And then let go: let go of your self to meet them in a communal space. Search for evidence of their unique truth and goodness. Stay focused on *them*.

If, in the moment, you feel overwhelmed or need time to complete the process, repeat their name to confirm it. Then, drawing a breath, seal it in.

Let go to be present

When do you feel most alive? This question was recently posed to a group of successful business leaders from many different backgrounds. Their responses included

- being outdoors in nature,
- playing with their children,
- listening to music,
- working on an inspiring project, and
- relaxing on vacation.

The moments they cited touched upon many different aspects of their lives. Sometimes they were alone; sometimes they were interacting with someone else, and sometimes they were focused on a particular activity.

When asked *what* they felt during these moments, their responses were startlingly similar:

"I felt really focused."

"I felt deeply connected to someone I care about."

"I felt as though I lost track of time."

In other words, while the activities varied, the experience was the same: they were at once fully engaged in the moment and free from any distraction. They felt alive.

When we reflect on vibrant and vital experiences in our own lives, we notice they are not always related to a specific place, person, or event; they change over time. But they are always characterized by a feeling of complete absorption in the moment, by the falling away of a world not related to the focus of our attention. We are not only focused on the object, person, or task in front of us—we have our hearts in it. In other words, we know that the moment has our full attention when we feel our hearts in a state of harmonic flow.

So what keeps us from investing that same care and curiosity in every part of our lives? Maybe we relate to this moment as merely a step to somewhere else. Or maybe we are listening to the voice of dissatisfaction perpetually whining *if only: If only I had more time. If only I had the courage. If only things would go my way.* Our attitudes sculpt the shape of our experience—the result informed by the degree to which we are willing to live with uncertainty.

Let's say you form the intention to spend time with someone you care about. You pick a night to go out together to your favorite restaurant, but when you get there, it is closed and your expectations are confounded. Will you spend the rest of the evening dismayed, thinking your plans have been ruined? Or will you choose to pass the evening enjoying each other's company in a more spontaneous way? In focusing on your intentions rather than expectations, you can embrace whatever arises in the moment.

Let go of the past: the achievements and joys, as well as the disappointments, wounds, and wanting things to be different. Learn from the past, accept it, and then let it go. Don't let memories bully you or seduce you into forgetting that your life is passing by *now*. Close the door on yesterday or condemn yourself to repeating it.

Let go of wanting. Wanting, both to have and *not* to have, is unhealthy; it leads only to more wanting. True want points toward a *need*. Needs alert us to the absence of something vital; they summon us to action until they are satisfied. Wants, on the other hand, are phantoms of the mind. They dissolve in the harmonic flow, receding when we lose ourselves in life. Whenever want arises, separate the negative desire from the positive intentions that point toward an underlying need. Focus on relieving the unmet condition or satisfying the unfulfilled possibility. Then let go.

Let go of hate. Hate is a disease, and in its many forms—anger, judgment, and fear—it will sicken its host. Relieve it with the antidotes of curiosity and compassion.

Let go to forgive

When necessary, forgive. The hot coal burns only the hand of the one holding it. Sometimes, letting go requires us to forgive what seems unforgiveable. Holding anger robs us of our right minds, blinding us to what is true, hurting us physically, emotionally, and mentally.

As the artist and writer C. R. Strahan said, "Forgiveness has nothing to do with absolving a criminal of his crime. It has everything to do with relieving oneself of the burden of being a victim—letting go of the pain and transforming oneself from victim to survivor."

Here is a secret. It can save you if you enter into it completely: every step we took in the past was a step toward this place, where we are just now. This moment is perfect just as it is; it becomes imperfect only when we attempt to make it something different. Remaining completely present—emptying ourselves of always already knowing—we may experience the sublime in the here and now. Just repeat to yourself,

present moment, only moment;
present moment, perfect moment.

Choosing to be present naturally draws you into synchrony with the object, person, or task before you. When your senses become saturated with sights, sounds, smells, and tastes, yesterday's stories fall away, along with any anxiety about the future. And in this ripe moment lies the key to not only greater awareness but to unlocking the happiness within.

Perspective

The mirror is not you. The mirror is you looking at yourself. — George Balanchine

Consider the person you know best: yourself. What picture do you see in your mind? Chances are, you're imagining a reflection of yourself in a mirror. But how accurate is it? The mirror offers only a reverse image of real life. Moreover, it reflects you in two dimensions, a flattened image that grows larger or smaller based on our relative distance to it. What do you look like from the side or from behind? How about from above or below? Even our physical presence has more dimensions than we can see on our own—we are more like a statue than a picture.

Walking around the statue

To truly appreciate a statue, one must walk around it and study it from all angles. Notice the space it inhabits, how light responds to it, and its relationship to the objects in its surroundings. Now visualize watching yourself from some distance. What is your relationship to the objects and people around you? As your field of view expands, notice how it feels. It feels better. The deeper your perspective, the greater your ability to see connectedness. With increasing distance, opportunities expand, challenges diminish, and connections appear limitless.

Even the perspectives we hold as irrefutable are often only preferences that skew the way we approach every occasion. "Anchovies taste terrible. Obviously everyone else must hate them too. Who would eat a pizza covered with salty fish?" But stores and restaurants keep offering them, so it seems reasonable that someone must like them. If you can imagine a world where at least one other person enjoys anchovies, then it cannot be true (a whole truth) that everyone dislikes anchovies.

It may at first be confusing to entertain views contrary to our fundamental beliefs, that other perspectives may be as valid as those we are committed to. While we might long for absolutes and be adamant that these differences exist, most are artificial distinctions, like marks on a clock or boundaries on a map. To question the assumptions that inform our beliefs is healthy. Beliefs, *especially* long-held beliefs, form the boundaries of our environment. How often do we sift through the facts that underlie their premises?

Consider Martin, who a few months ago ended a relationship with Diane because he felt she ignored his feelings. Not long after, he began dating Helen and was convinced she was the one. When you next run into him and the conversation turns to his relationship with Helen, you are less than completely surprised to hear that Martin, once again, feels the woman in his life ignores his feelings, is selfish, lacks compassion, and so on.

Although Martin believes that Diane and Helen, and possibly all women, have little regard for his feelings, the truth is, Martin simply fails to tell them what his feelings are. In fact, Martin is afraid that if he dares assert himself, the woman in his life will leave him. By giving in to this fear, Martin guarantees he will always date women who do not fulfill his desires (nor he theirs). To break the cycle, he must be willing to initiate a conversation about the relationship he desires, to say what he wants, and to learn how *she* feels about the life he imagines.

Martin's story emphasizes how a limited perspective can lead to unfortunate or even tragic consequences; we repeat the same mistakes until we are willing to learn from others how what *we* want resembles what *they* want. Inviting others into the inquiry, we explore how their perspectives influence our own. Even if we remain focused on our ideal, it's helpful to continue asking ourselves, what point of view am I holding? and what other points of view are possible? Developing a habit of second-guessing our assumptions disrupts our routine patterns and provides revelations that expand our horizons. Doing so invites us to reimagine our dreams—to integrate and transform both theirs and ours.

Be aware of your emotional state

Emotions are natural, instinctive, and essential for human survival. They teach us how the inner world meets the outer world, and that our response to the environment matters. Unlike sensations, which reflect our conscious experience, emotions are the initial interpretation of our sensations. They color our relationship with reality and inform how we feel.

Because we are emotional beings, we attach meaning to almost everything we encounter. Our response to the unforeseen is immediate and sometimes intense, ranging from curiosity to fear. Depending on the feelings aroused, the meaning we attach to the object or situation may be as simple as like, dislike, or indifference. In the same moment we filter our awareness, we anticipate how we *might* feel, judging what we will embrace and what we will avoid. Later, encountering the familiar, we blunt the full impact of a similar experience by relying on what we think we already know: *been there, done that.*

Distinguishing elements of our emotional composition can illuminate the changing nature of our beliefs, especially, for example, when we face challenges or unexpected departures from familiar conventions. Sometimes our first response to these encounters is confusing and hard to assimilate, an overwhelming sensation that gives rise to anxiety, worry, and doubt. When this happens, stop, step back, and take a breath. What are you responding to? within yourself? within your environment?

Consider the wisest people you know—those you turn to for advice. Imagine what they might suggest to liberate you from the tensions of an imaginary or artificial crisis. "Will this pass or does it point to a pattern?" Or maybe they would say something simple: "slow down," "look at the bigger picture," or "what really matters?" Sometimes, during truly critical intervals, what they offer is far simpler—their presence, wordless, subtle, and warm, probably their most valuable gift to us. The serenity and wisdom of their being.

Every situation is novel. While no one can control what emotions arise in any given moment, we can learn to remain dispassionate and observe our responses without acting on them. Approaching each experience with a willingness to learn we see farther and take on perspectives that both liberate us and make for a richer present. To the degree that we remain open in this way, we become sensitive to the potential in each moment even as we lose ourselves in the rhythm of life.

Practice mindfulness

How then do we voluntarily opt into this state of harmonic flow, even as we maintain unwavering focus on our tasks? *Mindfulness.*

To cultivate mindfulness, try this just now: Give yourself ten minutes or so during which there is nowhere to go and nothing to do. During this time try simply to "let go." "Do" nothing but be aware—of your body, heart, and mind. Just notice.

As distractions arise, do not deny them; resistance only increases their hold. Just observe them—and label them if you must: *voice of hunger, voice of planning,* or *voice of worry*; or simply *hunger, planning,* or *worrying*—and let them be. If the distraction is a task, then commit it to a list if you must. Most important, give yourself permission to just be present to the moment. This is mindfulness.

Whatever the reason, many of us resist dedicating time to practicing mindfulness. Maybe some of us feel that real life must be put on hold *before* we can indulge in what seems like an exotic experiment. In fact, at first, almost everyone is excruciatingly aware of usual consciousness impatiently tapping its foot and glancing at its watch.

But if we're willing to stop long enough to surrender to it, unstructured time can be a reward, an extraordinary portal to the sublime and the deepest levels of truth. In such moments of being, we discover thoughts floating into awareness like clouds taking form in the sky. Over time, we learn to observe distractions and let them go. And with perseverance, as the mirage of identity dissolves, we may gradually become aware of the expression of the divine passing through us. In this relaxed state, we can linger and examine our thoughts, gain insight into the self, and form a better relationship with our emotions.

Mindfulness is not so much a goal as a state of awareness—like a clear, spacious expanse of sky. It does not choose the placement of the sun or the moon and is indifferent to wind or rain. It remains neutral. Its equal partner, concentration, provides a magnifying glass to more closely examine the objects within the atmosphere of our choosing. Concentration provides the discipline for learning, even complex learning, and the mental stamina required for transformation.

If they are to benefit us properly, mindfulness and concentration must be used flexibly—one or the other predominating as the occasion warrants. In the extreme, too much mindfulness leads to apathy. In the euphoria of unbounded awareness, it is easy to lose sight of our needs or those of others. Similarly, too great a concentration can lead to obsession, a fanatic focusing on whatever claims our attention. Unchecked, the flame of concentration reduces everything to ashes. But when harmoniously balanced, mindfulness and concentration set us free, allowing us to let go and see what really matters.

Looking back on the study of the seminary students, the subtle aspects of the circumstances contributed to a wide disparity in behavior. One of the psychologists' findings was that students who were told to hurry were less prone to provide help than those who were told they had additional time, and those who were asked to talk about the parable of the Good Samaritan were more likely to give assistance than those providing career advice.[17] When the impact of personality type was compared with context (whether they perceived themselves to be in a hurry or whether they were thinking about a relevant parable), the effect of individual intensity of religious belief was almost insignificant. In this context, the situation easily trumped personality.

One might imagine that seminary students are relatively more compassionate than the average college student.

Perhaps they are. Nevertheless, even seminary students gave in to the pressure of a deadline and their fear of disapproval to the degree that they ignored a human being apparently in desperate need of medical attention. Had they been capable of recognizing their emotional responses and practiced in the art of watching those emotions dissipate, they might have been better able to understand what response was called for in the moment.

Mindfulness helps us discern the nature of emotions. In the deepest states of mindfulness, we can see the true nature of our thoughts or emotions, and even sever the roots of those we cannot otherwise let go of. Emancipating us from reactionary responses, mindfulness is the best strategy for opting into a state of harmonic flow or, more simply, for feeling alive.

Chapter 9 Summary: *Let Go* advocates that we be our best selves in the present

Planning liberates your attention. Letting go allows you to focus on right thoughts, words, and actions—to respond to the real needs of the moment.

There is a certain grace in letting go. It allows us to accept what is and what isn't. So much of life is habit; the habits formed by routinely living into a life plan eliminate the uncertainty of where, how, and what, freeing us to relax and savor the experience of each step we take. Moreover, with our minds unencumbered, we react intuitively amid ever-changing circumstances. Letting go, we connect with our "whole intelligence," the complementary interaction of our sensory, emotional, and cognitive awareness. By applying our whole intelligence to experience, we enjoy a depth of perspective that reveals opportunities invisible to a less flexible mind. Letting go sounds easy. But the modern world is filled with innumerable distractions that inhibit our ability to be present in the moment. Letting go frees us from fear, greed, and delusion so we may live with things just as they are.

The path to letting go is *posture, presence,* and *perspective.*

Posture

- Survey your body—how you stand, and how you face any situation.
- Reconnect to your senses: Look. Listen. Touch. Smell. Taste. Remember these first teachers.
- Distinguish between healthy and unhealthy tension: healthy tension sharpens focus; unhealthy tension (too much tension), however, produces anxiety or even chronic stress.

- Counter tension by identifying where it is stored, breathing deeply, and releasing it.

Presence

- Be present to overcome small complaints of the mind that distract you from the moment.
- Let go of stories, disappointments, wounds, and wanting the past to be different. When necessary, forgive.
- Shed the armor of identity; realize the gift of another's presence and connect directly with each unforgettably vivid human being.
- Engage in the moment. Notice how you feel as everything else falls away.
- Forget the small self. Forgetting is the gateway to immersion in the harmonic flow.

Perspective

- "Walk around the statue" to heighten situational awareness. Seeing things from as many angles as possible, you learn that all points of view are relative and limited.
- Widen your perspective to better respond to the needs of the moment.
- Let go using mindfulness and concentration. Mindfulness is naked awareness—the delicate state that precedes thinking. Concentration is focus unimpeded by reflection, analysis, or comparison.
- Free yourself to dissolve into experience as you enter the flow.

CHAPTER 10. CHOOSE LOVE

Every man builds his world in his own image. He has the power to choose, but no power to escape the necessity of choice. — Ayn Rand

Paul was a stockbroker. While his father had been a journalist, his family was proud of Paul's desire to succeed in business. In time, he married a young woman and they settled down to have a family, comfortable with the steady income his work provided. What Paul really loved, though, was art. Although his career was taking off, nothing made him feel more alive than standing with a brush in hand, absorbed in transferring his vision onto a canvas in bold, saturated colors. Paul spent weekends painting and seeking out other painters to learn from. For a decade, he lived a divided life: working all week to make money; living into his passion at nights and on weekends.

One day, after eleven years in business, Paul quit his day job to dedicate himself to painting. In short order, his financial position changed dramatically, and Paul and his family moved from their comfortable home to an apartment. Regardless, Paul was happy; feeling a deepening connectedness to his work, he even began to hold showings of his paintings in the family's small apartment.

But for Paul's wife, the artist's life was unfulfilling. The marriage faltered, and eventually she left, taking their five children. Not long after, Paul moved to the coast, withdrawing from the city life he felt pressured him to be "artificial and conventional." What friends he had made in the business world abandoned him.

Finding the simple life nourishing to his spirit, Paul found his way to an island, where he spent much of the rest of his life. There, he continued to paint, though his art was not widely appreciated, nor did it provide significant income. But Paul remained committed to his art, and his passion flowed into his painting. Virtually unknown and in relative poverty, he died at only 54.

Following his death, those painters he had studied with and had invited to his apartment so many years earlier began to reevaluate his work. They and many subsequent reviewers belatedly came to appreciate Paul as a true original and a genius in his own way. Fortunately for us all, Paul's very obscurity during his lifetime and his remote South Sea location resulted in the preservation of most of his work. Indeed, today we can still see original paintings he made on the islands, because Paul's last name was Gauguin, and his paintings share space alongside the works of such masters as Picasso and van Gogh in the great museums of the world.

Gauguin's life was not always filled with joy. During many periods of darkness, he wrestled with the direction of his life and struggled to maintain his commitment to a calling that did not provide financial success. And while one might question the morality of his putting work before duty to his family, it is indisputable that he found his true calling. Whatever his shortcomings as a husband and father, Paul lived into his purpose by pursuing what he loved the most. To do so, he was forced to abandon a world he found sterile, colorless, and stifled by convention. But this very wholehearted commitment produced a legacy of vivid, symbolic paintings that expressed a passion for everything vibrant, natural, and sensuous.

The fifth inquiry addresses the question of how we become our greatest selves.

The answer is really very simple: choose love.

Who you are and your happiness both reflect a history of choices affecting your relationship with your self, others, the present, and the future. Change is the world bringing something to us. Choice is our opportunity to give something back. Thus, as we *co-create* the world, the secret to wholeness and happiness is hidden in plain sight: choose love in each thought, word, and action. Love is the product of all wisdom. Choosing love reveals authentic purpose, leads to wholeness, and liberates the best you—the person you are meant to be.

This is the dilemma of freedom: because we are free to choose, we must accept responsibility for the choices we make. To see things otherwise is to deny what is real, to renounce freedom, and to allow life to happen to us. If you're happy with all aspects of your life, why change? But if you're haunted by the past, afraid of the future, or nagged by dissatisfaction, lamenting unfulfilled potential, remember that the ever-changing nature of our existence presents us with a continuous stream of options. Each passing moment offers the opportunity to start anew. What you choose is what you get (WYCIWYG).

As the example of Gauguin demonstrates, living into your purpose means choosing to be what you love—every choice leading you closer to or farther away from what you love. Although the effects of your choices are not always deliberate or visible, the present moment discloses the influence of each one, large or small, intentional or inadvertent—a long-vanished butterfly whose wings stirred the wind that roiled the waves breaking now on *this* far-away shore. Thus, at its essence, the degree to which you fulfill your potential is inextricably linked to your choices. Descartes's famous dictum might as well have been: *I choose therefore I am.*

When we study the lives of those who have aspired to greatness, it becomes clear that *their* greatness was a product of their choices. Such extraordinary people share the following characteristics:

- They *committed* their lives to something greater than themselves.
- They *challenged* themselves and others to be their best.
- They *chose* to bring wholeness to each of the domains of their lives, to self, to others, to the future, and to the present moment.

Such men and women consciously dedicate their individual strengths to a communal purpose, deliberately casting away relics of identity no longer essential to their general wellbeing in favor of the collective good. Such maturity is not conferred by the attainment of a certain age or status; it is the voluntary disposition to sacrifice what you want for what you know is right. These individuals are quietly prepared to sacrifice their own desires in favor of something bigger: a loved one, a family, or a cause committed to creating a better world. Such people verify the assertion that happiness and feeling alive are byproducts of remaining focused on a goal beyond mere gratification of their own wants. In them we observe a will to grow into an awareness that extends beyond the sphere of the small self—a prerequisite for greatness.

While circumstances of time and place may have propelled them to fame, all great men and women became great by losing themselves in the love of something transcendent. And the same spark that ignited their greatness exists within us all. As Jean Houston suggests, "The universe is holding its breath, waiting for you to take your place."

Commit

I'd rather attempt to do something great and fail than to attempt to do nothing and succeed. —Robert Schuller

Whatever we believe we *cannot* do, we cannot do. Whatever we think we *can* do, we can—once we commit our bodies, hearts, and minds to making it so.

Commitment: a promise brought into being

To commit means to promise to either *do* something or *not do* something. As individuals, we may express our commitments publicly in the form of a vow, pledge, or resolution. When two or more people exchange commitments, a bond is created between them.

Whether consciously or unconsciously declared, our commitments permeate us, define what we stand for, what we will *not* stand for, what we will sacrifice for and, in some cases, what we are willing to die for. Our commitments define our relationships to others through our moral and ethical state of being—our character.

Sometimes we confuse a commitment with a goal. Finishing school, making a million dollars, or contributing a portion of your income to charity are all admirable goals, but they are not commitments. The difference is that a commitment is an act of devotion intended to foster or promote a general (sometimes future) condition, such as living a healthy lifestyle or ending homelessness, whereas as a goal defines a specific milestone marking the progress of living into a commitment. Commitments embrace a willingness to remain constant in the face of uncertainty and to sacrifice one's own individual, egoic interests in favor of a larger shared purpose. A commitment consumes all doubt.

Regardless of one's attitude toward the military and the uses it has been put to at times, most people can agree that an organization that embodies commitment in its purest form is the US Marine Corps. As America's force in readiness, members of the Corps are distinguished by their dedication to discipline, their commitment to fulfilling their missions, and their unsurpassed patriotism. While many organizations offer a career, the Marine Corps promises "a new life." The process of beginning that new life as a member of the Marine Corps begins with a commitment. Each new cadet commits his fidelity to the Marine Corps and, in return, the Marine Corps offers a reciprocal commitment of fidelity to the marine—*semper fidelis*, always faithful. This institutionalized expression of mutual commitment can be a transformative event. By making a commitment to the Corps, each marine becomes part of something greater. Ask any marine what he or she values, and the answers will include such words as honor, loyalty, and dedication. The ideals they cherish—God, Country, Corps, Family, and Self, in that order—take precedence over their own selfish interests.

Every marine knows their country relies on them to protect it, and the Corps relies upon them to serve it. Although few marines actually enjoy getting up at dawn and running ten miles to stay fit, they do it anyway, knowing they could be called on tomorrow to take up arms against an enemy in combat. Every marine—as well as the many other dedicated warriors who serve their country—is willing to put themselves in harm's way to protect their countrymen and their fellow marines. Most of us can only wonder what it feels like to live with such a fierce, clear commitment. By committing themselves, new marines begin to realize the possibility of a new life. Paradoxically perhaps, they feel an intense vitality the moment they adopt the warrior way of life and sincerely put their country and the Corps above themselves. We all want to feel more alive, and for a marine that feeling of vitality increases every day he serves the Corps.

Commit to something greater

So what are you committed to? What makes you feel more alive? Commitments come in all forms. They don't always require such a serious and solemn act as joining the US Marines. Commitment is a habit of living into our guiding principles until they become a natural way of being.

Sometimes commitments are more noticeable by their breach. Perhaps contrary to your promises you have let your health slide and are now suffering medical consequences. Perhaps your devotion to a relationship faltered such that it eroded or broke apart, or maybe your commitment to work has weakened and your performance has suffered. Wherever you experience a loss of enthusiasm in fulfilling your responsibilities, take note.

This malaise is often a symptom that you may need to re-evaluate your commitment within the context of the present state of your life. Is it one you still endorse or accept? If it is, then maybe you've drifted out of alignment with something you value, and need to reset the course. Alternatively, such internal resistance may indicate that priorities have changed, that you may be trying to uphold ideals you don't truly believe in or you are now beginning to question. In any case, it is almost always true that you have difficulty sustaining commitments when you have not been completely honest with yourself.

Our most successful commitments arise from moving *toward* happiness, rather than *away from* the things we intend to avoid. Negative commitments—oaths we swear, for example, not to be like our parents, not to depend on anyone, never again to leave ourselves emotionally vulnerable—are not commitments to something greater; they do nothing to help us feel more alive. By their nature, negative commitments are the reactionary fragments of an unlived life. At their core, they reflect *patterns of aversion*—an unconscious willingness to settle for a life unfulfilled.

So much of life is a habit. Until the day comes when you make that big commitment, you can still move your life in the right direction by honoring small, daily commitments. Such commitments can be as simple as making time in our mornings to listen to the voice of wisdom, writing down our goals for the day, or simply resolving to keep our word. The habit of making and keeping principled commitments will serve you well when the day arrives for your purpose to come into focus and you see what you were born to do—your path to greatness.

Commit to Love

Stories of superheroes exist not to make us believe that the world is a scary place but to convince us that maybe we have the potential to fly. Imagine a comic book hero based on your own life. What superpowers would you choose? There's Batman, a master of martial arts with an impressive arsenal of tactical gear. Then there is the Green Lantern, who has a power ring that will amplify the power of its wearer; and Aquaman, who can swim really fast and talk to fish.

But there is one superhero who stands above them all: Superman. He is "faster than a speeding bullet, more powerful than a locomotive, and able to leap tall buildings in a single bound." Drawing on his array of superpowers, Superman is able to single-handedly conquer the strongest of evildoers and has been credited with everything from stopping a runaway train to saving us all from a meteor on a cataclysmic path toward the planet. Given all his strengths, who wouldn't want to be Superman?

A good Batman story is entertaining and leaves you thinking, *Batman is cool.* A good Green Lantern story is generally fraught with peril but, in the end, we only wish we had a power ring. But a Superman story fills us with awe. Every day, we turn on the TV and hear bad news about people doing terrible things to each other. On the worst days, we might wonder whether people are inherently evil or whether there might not be something wrong deep down in the human heart. And then along comes Superman, gazing upon the world with compassion, consumed with the unfathomable belief that if we understood our potential, we would never raise a hand in anger toward one another again.

So what is the source of Superman's powers? The sun. The solar energy of the sun is a force stronger than any other on earth . . . except one.

There is one power known to man that "knows no limit to its endurance, no end to its trust, no fading of its hope; outlasts anything; and still stands when all else has fallen."[18] It is a force greater than any other that brings out the Superman or Superwoman in each of us.

And what is this power? Of course, it is Love.

It is the one power above all others. Consider all that has been accomplished in the name of love. What other force unites our bodies, hearts, and minds and connects us with every other living being? Though we associate it with vulnerability, in truth, love is the source of our greatest strength.

As we speak of "love," the word itself serves as a proxy for the sublime expression of the divine in us, between us, and around us. It is the medium through which we access *what is*—awareness—and realize *what is possible*—wholeness and happiness. Whether you subscribe to a particular religion, find communion in nature, or even reject all belief systems, there is no denying that something connects us all in a way beyond our ability to describe in mere words. This power can be best expressed as love.[19]

And if "love" is not the word for you, then choose the one most important to you, whether it is god, family, success, happiness, or some other word that resonates within you. When you find this word, you discover a way of accessing the greatest force in the universe, your own inexhaustible reservoir of strength. Imagine now what you might be capable of.

Superman did not get to choose the source of his power, but you can. Like the sun, love is an unlimited source of energy. If you try to observe it directly it overwhelms the senses, yet you are always aware of its presence; you sense the warmth of its fire and observe the radiance of its light in everything around you. Put simply, love is the ultimate superpower. And once you commit to love, you too will believe a man can fly.

Challenge

Being deeply loved by someone gives you strength, while loving someone deeply gives you courage. —Lao Tzu

One would think our first commitment should be to ourselves, to being up front about who we are and refusing to disguise or compromise what we stand for. While being true to ourselves frees us to live unapologetically and, so, more authentically and effectively, the real stakes are much higher. Being our *best* self requires a commitment to something or someone we love and bringing forward the fullest expression of our being—being willing to sacrifice who we think we are for what we know is right.

Challenge your self to be your best self

It is vital to have a healthy sense of self—strong individual purpose, values, and commitment. But a limited "I, me, my" perspective obstructs our view of reality, leaving us unable to see what does not appear to affect us directly. Letting go of the small self—the part of us whose main concern is manufacturing distinctions to preserve the status quo—is the key to becoming your authentic, best self. Whenever the small self senses a threat, it clings to the identity it has created, surrounding it with drama and casting us in the lead role of a show entitled *All About Me*. In fact, if your life seems like a soap opera, it probably is. Breaking the addiction and ending the cycle of drama requires not only commitment but the courage to challenge your very perception of who you are.

Pain and anger can be harnessed to actualize what is possible on our journey toward a healthier way of being. If, despite months or years of your best efforts, peace and satisfaction still elude you, it is probably time to ask yourself what aspect of reality you are resisting. The chance to be happy often requires being willing to do exactly what we are deeply committed to in body, heart, and mind. Conversely, the unwillingness to risk dissolving a static identity—an unwillingness to learn and change—may be the very thing that keeps us from being truly happy. This realization can motivate us to summon the courage to sacrifice whatever stands between us and contentment—including the small self.

On those days you have fallen short of being your best, let that go too. Begin the next day with renewed commitment. The challenge is to be your best from day to day, even in the face of others' disappointment or disapproval. Some people may not agree with what you stand for—and sometimes, your truth causes them to question their own way of being. But if you consistently act with integrity, you often discover that people are drawn to such honesty. Honesty creates trust. Being true to your own nature frees others to be themselves as well.

Take Harry for example: Harry suffered from prostate cancer. He was embarrassed about it and felt as if it undermined his manhood. Moreover, he feared his friends would shun him and that he could no longer have a relationship with a woman. But he was more committed to honesty than to holding on to a false image of masculinity. So when people questioned him about his illness, instead of evading the question or lying, he answered their questions honestly. Other men whose experiences were similar but who were afraid to talk about them were encouraged by Harry's honesty and found it easier to open up and tell their own stories. They were grateful and relieved to finally be able to share their own challenges with a veteran of the same war.

Harry found relief in laying himself bare to what he feared the most—being rejected by his friends. To his surprise, his very openness elicited empathy and candor from those whose stories and experiences mirrored his own but who had never before found the courage to speak of them. Harry's own process of healing healed others, and, in their own sharing, they helped heal him.

Living into being our authentic (best) selves, we encounter people who need us to show up so *they* can show up. Until now, they hadn't shown up because *we* hadn't.

A measure of your own commitment to something larger than yourself is your willingness to stand in the fire of self-sacrifice. It may mean losing friends, a certain lifestyle, and many of the things by which you have come to identify yourself. It is a willingness to surrender to the light so that what is loving and selfless can emerge. Often this means that the world into which this larger being emerges will differ from the one you are used to.

It is natural to run away from a fire. But those who are willing to run toward the flames are the people who change the world.

Challenge yourself to love unconditionally

We already know it, but it is worth periodically reminding ourselves that the ability to extend love to others grows from having learned how to love ourselves—to find compassion in the face of our differences without condemning them. By acknowledging our own failings rather than trying to disguise or ignore them, we see things more clearly and find opportunities to make choices truly aligned with our purpose and values. "People are often unreasonable, irrational, and self-centered," notes Kent Keith. "Love them anyway." This means loving ourselves too.

Perhaps it feels difficult to offer yourself love. Yet it is a particularly powerful practice. The more you accept the person whose flaws you know best, even those you're trying to correct, the less you will find to condemn in others. Only through showing yourself compassion will you cultivate the loving-kindness to share with strangers.

Becoming kinder and more compassionate means loving others just as they are. While it might be natural to notice flaws and imperfections or to feel compelled to tell others what they shouldn't be doing, remember that people usually do what's right when they can see what the right thing is. Too often we criticize others for the absence of what we believe is possible, something that rarely leads to change when an investment of thoughtful care instead would make things better. If we can catch ourselves before blurting out something harmful, we may benefit from insight into what is motivating us to be critical. The sooner we recognize conditioned reflexes for what they are, the sooner we can let them go and get back to illuminating the best in others through extending unconditional love.

What does it mean to love someone unconditionally? Ken Wilber, the author and proponent of Integral Theory, describes unconditional love this way:

> Love until it hurts, love to infinity, love until there is no me left anywhere, only this radiant living Thou who bestows all glory, all goods, all knowledge, all grace, and forgives me deeply for my own manifestation, which inherently brings suffering to others, but which the loving God of the thou-ness of this moment can and does release, forgive, heal and make whole . . . but only if I can deeply and radically surrender in love and devotion to the Great-Thou dimension of this now.[20]

Until the people in our lives are relieved of the responsibility to make us happy, they will grow no further. To love them is to accept them unconditionally, to prize their differences, and continue loving them *as they are* without imposing our own wants or needs or expectations—even when they make choices that deny their own beauty, truth, and goodness.

Without such love, our loved ones are as likely to make life-altering changes as a night-blooming flower is to bloom at midday. Any expression of disapproval or judgment on our part serves only to make others shut down and take cover from the cold.

Challenge yourself to love those close to you unconditionally regardless of circumstances. Indeed, often this is the most important role you can play for a loved one: to see their true potential, even when they can't see it—a better relationship, a better career, greater happiness, or liberation from their own self-limiting fears. Loving them this way creates a holistic relationship between a lover and beloved.

Seeing the best in others, you bring forward the best part of yourself as well.

Whenever you're tempted to try to change someone, stop and ask yourself why: Whose needs or desires are you responding to? It is essential to evaluate your own motivations and ensure that you are not offering help or advice to seek something in return. Quite simply, be clear that are you are helping people in ways they have *asked* to be helped. If you can't articulate a clear connection between your aid and their requests, consider whether you are imposing your own ambitions or preferences on others.

Real positive change comes from within. To make a fundamental change, *you* must want to change, just as *they* must. As painful as it may be to witness, you cannot save a person deeply committed to drowning. Appointing yourself as the lifeguard only endangers your own life.

Neil is a good example of someone unwittingly committed to a path of self-destruction. A doctor turned administrator, Neil was dedicated to creating seamless consistency in the delivery of health care. But despite professional success, he struggled with his personal life. His hypercritical regard extended beyond the medical system to include himself and the people closest to him. Wherever he looked he perceived flaws, and a cloud of self-loathing and disapproval surrounded him. His family and friends even began to jokingly call him "Negative Neil."

Rather than acknowledge and learn to make peace with his critical nature, he turned to alcohol. And briefly, it worked; drinking silenced the critical voice in his mind. But his attempt to relieve stress with alcohol quickly became unmanageable, and Neil found himself on an accelerating downward spiral. Recognizing that he was on a destructive path, Neil's family and friends tried to persuade him to stop, even threatening to shun him if he would not. He responded by quitting drinking for a day, sometimes several days, but then he would start again. Neil was slowly drowning himself.

After about a year, he hit bottom. The once high-flying professional was broke and nearly homeless. On the brink of losing everything and everybody, Neil gave in and entered a rehab program. But the sobriety would not last, because he was still unable to see that alcohol was just a symptom. The real problem was his unwillingness to confront his compulsive urge to find fault. What was the origin of this anxiety? Although he clearly needed to quit drinking, his deeper need was to understand how to dissolve an ingrained negativity toward others and see how certain processes benefited from his critical evaluation while the people surrounding him did not. Doing so, he might commit to appreciating the value of individuality, and understand that differences are often strengths rather than flaws. Moreover, *he* had to want to change. Although his friends could reflect the possibilities they saw in him as a dedicated physician, only he could make the necessary transformation. In the end, Neil's opinion of himself was the one that mattered most.

Like Neil, people are often desperately trying to save their own lives and overcome their fears. Neil wanted to believe that his life had value, but he was also committed to a view that he was unworthy. He was unable to recognize that all his complaints were negative expressions of his urge to make the world a better place. Neil and many of us like him are unable to voice our wishes in a positive way,

THE POWER OF 10

because we're afraid of exposing our vulnerabilities. We long for warmth, compassion, care, respect, cooperation, and collaboration. But our frustrations and anger drive others away, sealing us off from the contact that might break the cycle.

Until Neil was able to seize the opportunity to create something affirmative and new that made use of his unique talents, he felt trapped in the half-light. Focused critically *inward* instead of compassionately *outward*, all he could see was his own shadows.

Every one of us dreads seeing someone we care about going through a period of darkness. Though we instinctively want to help, *pushing* usually leads to rebellion. But the light of unconditional love *pulls* people forward. Recognizing the better nature within themselves, they voluntarily fulfill the possibility of what can be. As Goethe put it, "Treat a man as he appears to be, and you make him worse. But treat a man as if he already were what he potentially could be, and you make him what he should be."

Challenge your beliefs and perspective

The world is made up of stories. The stories we tell ourselves either lift us up or represent psychological barriers that suppress our potential.

In his commencement address to the graduates of Kenyon College, author David Foster Wallace described the value of perspective this way: "There are these two young fish swimming along and they happen to meet an older fish swimming the other way, who nods at them and says, 'Morning, boys. How's the water?' And the two young fish swim on for a bit, and then eventually one of them looks over at the other and asks, 'What the hell is water?'"

Consider some of the things you may take for granted about yourself—perhaps you are introverted or extroverted, live in a certain kind of place, have certain friends, do a certain work, have your *own* general sense of the world. If everything is the product of choice, when and how did you make those choices? How many of them were made freely, after you developed the ability to understand what those choices meant? Examining the patterns in your life provides a clearer grasp of the beliefs and perspectives that inform the choices you make. Yet we rarely question them. They feel as natural as being left or right handed, but they are not necessarily natural or even true.

Think of some beliefs you had in the past that you have since rejected: Monsters live under your bed or in your closet. If you cross your eyes, they might get stuck. Babies are the result of French kissing. Beliefs like these undoubtedly influenced you as a child. Even now, as an adult, you likely hold other beliefs that are only marginally less outlandish. You might, for example, believe you could never learn Chinese. But if you lived in China for any length of time, no such belief in your own incapacity would arise.

When we believe something to be true, we make it so, often unconsciously. When we fear something, we are liable to spend our lives avoiding it while failing to examine the underlying fear.

Most of our fears are rooted in distorted beliefs formed when we were young and dependent on others for our basic needs. Many of us felt deeply vulnerable because of our dependency on those we needed to care for us. Our relationships with them held the threat, whether imaginary or real, of rejection, abandonment, or being turned away. We felt the potential loss of our caregivers' approval as a fundamental threat to our very survival. At such moments, we made a silent pledge to ourselves: conform to the desires of others or lose their protection.

From the day we understood that our survival depended on others, we began to think and act in ways we thought would reduce the risk of abandonment or rejection. We learned to censor our perceptions and filter them through the beliefs imposed on us. We trained ourselves to see scarcity where there was abundance, ascribed value based on acceptance instead of merit, and stopped living as independent beings. The more difficult the circumstances, the more we closed down and distanced ourselves from our true thoughts, words, and actions. In the simplest terms, many of us lived with our true nature shrouded in a protective layer of fear. Some of us still do. We live with the conviction that we are *not* okay while simultaneously seeking evidence to the contrary, in the forlorn hope that this idea might not be true.

Even the most confident among us vacillates between feelings of magnificence and abhorrence. Imagine the biggest, toughest person you know wearing a nametag: "Hello, my name is _____." In small print under their name is a disclaimer: "I want your acceptance more than anything in the world, and I am terrified that if you knew the real me you would not give it, because somewhere, somehow, someone I once depended on made me believe I was not good enough."

We imagine our feelings of inadequacy are deserved, which leads to self-loathing, delusions about our true nature and the desire to become someone else. These delusions are buried so deep in the subconscious that they continue to distort the way we think, speak, and act long after we have earned independence and have nothing to fear. While the actual threat may have subsided, the stories we tell ourselves can persist for a lifetime, causing us to create an unhealthy relationship with both self and others, as we hesitate and doubt ourselves just enough to keep success out of reach.

The persistence of this debilitating behavior is largely attributable to a reluctance to face our fears, and especially to our unwillingness to examine whether these fears are based on reality. Fear is almost never a response to what is actually happening in the moment but is usually apprehension of the unknown. But fear cannot grow unless we feed it. Fear is *not* the dark; it's just a scary story we tell ourselves about what *might happen* in the dark. Unless we are willing to free ourselves from our self-imposed boundaries and dare to be fearless and unguarded, we are destined to live small lives.

The challenge then is to identify and understand the competing beliefs and self-defeating stories that prevent us from taking risks. By digging down and illuminating their roots, we can rediscover the history and origins and underlying dispositions, both positive and negative. Once we know how our fears keep us from living into our potential, we must summon the courage to defy self-protective instincts—to *see* the limitations beliefs impose, and *see through* them. Imagine what the world would be like if these beliefs were true; then consider how to create something different *in spite of* the limitation. This flexibility has the potential to lead to revolutionary transformation—consistently engaging in conscious choices eventually gives way to new ways of being.

Like water to a fish, our invisible assumptions may be less a medium of propulsion than a viscous drag that holds us back. At some point so many years ago, at least one fish chose to challenge the status quo. Why not be the fish that emerges onto dry land and changes the world?

Choose

The content of your character is your choice. Day by day, what you choose, what you think, and what you do is who you become.
—Heraclitus

We often imagine going back in time, reliving a certain moment, and *this time* saying or doing the right thing. The French have an expression for this, *l'esprit d'escalier*—the spirit of the stairway, that describes realizing the right thing to say but only after a conversation has ended, presumably about the time we reach the bottom of the stairs on the way out.

Choose to honor the moment

By reflecting on our commitments and honoring this moment, we can avoid regret.

Each moment presents a choice. We can envision an intersection of paths leading in opposite directions: give or get, everything or nothing, work or rest, speak or listen, resist or surrender, fish or cut bait. The poles of a healthy dichotomy create an energy we can use for resolution, but which pole should we choose?

Often, both are correct, depending on the circumstances and timing. In the natural world, we might refer to this relativity as "the right season." There is a right time to plant, a right time to grow, and a right time to harvest. Rush any aspect of the process, and the fruit will not ripen. The present doesn't concern merely what I want or what you want but what the situation calls for in the moment.

Sometimes the moment calls for us to stand tall, such as when we witness oppression—or to be kind when we're tempted to lash out, such as during a disagreement with a friend or loved one. Whatever we choose determines whether we are moving toward or away from creating the life we want. We may not always *want* to do what the moment requires, but avoiding the call of the moment will have ramifications for us, our relationships, and our collective future. No one wants to wash the dishes after supper, but if not you or me, who? If not now, when? The opportunity for positive change is found inside the struggle, no matter how difficult it feels. The secret to unlocking change within yourself is to *want* what is on the other side of your commitment.

An unhealthy choice can feel satisfying in the moment but usually leaves a bad aftertaste. The right choice, on the other hand, can feel less satisfying when we make it but feels better and better with time. By focusing on our deeper *commitments*, we begin instinctively to *want* the feelings associated with choices that align with them. Over time this desire for integrity becomes stronger than the momentary fulfillment of a particular craving.

As you consider two extremes, as well as the field of possible choices between, it is important to remain focused on the positive intent: What would the *best you* do? Engage your voice of wisdom through your body, heart, and mind. Then choose to think, speak, and act as the best you. No regrets.

Letting go of any attachment to expectations is a critical element of building the right momentum and being willing to encounter the unexpected and learn something new. It is at once to grasp for what you desire *and* let go of the outcome.[21]

If you keep your intention to be your best self in the forefront of your mind and listen to your voice of wisdom, the best choices will reveal themselves. Recognizing the right choice is sometimes challenging, like groping through a bin full of avocados. To the inexperienced hand all avocados feel the same, but with practice you can learn to select just the right one.

Choose Wholeness

The people we most admire can often be described as *healthy* or *wholehearted* or *having high integrity.* Such people personify complete human beings with real substance. Indeed, the quality that unites all the diverse characteristics associated with such people is *wholeness.*

What is wholeness?

According to the dictionary, the word "wholeness" refers to something that is "complete or total." Applied to a person, it denotes "the entirety of a person's nature or development." In other words, wholeness is a state of being your *greatest self* in *all* the domains of your life. Simply put, wholeness is our highest aspiration.

If there were a measure for wholeness in our lives as there is for temperature, that measure would be happiness—a sustained wellbeing and vitality. By honestly surveying the areas in which you feel happiest, you sense wholeness. In contrast, areas in which you sense discontent suggest a lack of wholeness—a longing for the engagement of the full spectrum of your being.

Each of us is born with the potential to be whole. As intuitive and rational beings, we are also endowed with the power of choice and, being free to choose, intentionally and unintentionally, we make healthy and sometimes unhealthy choices. Unhealthy choices undermine our integrity and limit our potential. Wholeness, on the other hand, is the product of the tens, perhaps hundreds of *healthy* choices, each merging into the next, that permit us to see more deeply into reality. The deeper we see into reality, the more clearly we recognize that the two poles of existence—*what is* and *what is possible*—merge and unite through love. At the spark moment when we acknowledge our true nature, all fear falls away, and in its place is a deep, abiding peace.

In spite of uncertainty, we somehow know that cultivating the voice of wisdom helps us make the right choices. But how do we discern the positive from the negative expression of any given choice? We need only remember this essential truth: *the right choice is the one that brings more love into the world.* Often, we have no way of knowing whether a choice will ultimately have a positive or negative impact; however sincerely benevolent our motivations, the ripples of any act widen geometrically. Your voice of wisdom already knows this. Even the smallest selfless acts can influence your experience of the present as well as the future, benefiting the whole.

Choose Love

There is no greater or lesser expression of love; there is only love. Love is in us and surrounds us; we are particles of energy suspended in its light. We express love when we affirm it and surrender to it in the same moment.

Love is our partner, ally, and resource. It is the fundamental energy of life, the greatest of all superpowers. Love is not just a feeling or an achievement, and it is certainly not a trophy on the mantle. We do not fall in love; true love is the light of the divine flowing through us. Reducing the *resistance* to love is a continual practice, but *reconnecting* to love is immediate and direct: we sense it in our bodies, hold it in our hearts, and return to it in our minds.

Doubting love is easy; everyone questions whether it's real. But it is a false choice to conclude that there is either love or no love. While the rational mind may not fully comprehend it, the voice of wisdom confirms love's existence in the reflection of the beauty, truth, and goodness around us. Even in the midst of the most challenging circumstances, simply acknowledging our fear and looking for the points of light in the darkness where we *don't* feel afraid can guide us. We need only intensify this light by thinking, speaking, and acting with love. Love naturally illuminates the darkness and awakens the potential that has always been there. And now with both fear and love present, we can choose to focus on either the darkness or the light and, in choosing, to transcend suffering. In the words of Adyashanti, "The only residual suffering you feel is the love you withhold."

Taking a stand for love engenders a deep humility. True humility is not an unhealthy renunciation of the self; love acknowledges the oneness of all things without compromising individuality. Love unites all the domains of our lives, connecting the pauses between our breaths, the spaces between the beats of our hearts, and the intervals between our thoughts. It has the power of reunion to overcome estrangement, alienation, and loneliness. It is the unifying force of our interconnected world.

Finding love at the core of our being is the beginning of the end for everything in us that thinks it is separate. When we choose to think, speak, and act with love in all sincerity, we feel it—a vital force moving through us, transforming us, and reconstituting our being. And the more we allow love to flow through us, the less vulnerable we are to fear—a virtuous cycle that enriches our environment.

Each moment we surrender to and affirm love, we fulfill the potential within. As we do, our natural state of wholeness emerges—and happiness becomes our way of life.

So how do we become our greatest selves? Regardless of circumstances, choose love. *Omnia vincit amor*—love conquers all.

Chapter 10 Summary: *Choose Love* advocates that we intentionally choose love

Living into being our greatest selves means to choose love. Perhaps the most important element of this advocacy is commitment—a promise made to the divine spark that connects all living things, a dedication to the highest intention that a human being can express. This kind of commitment is transformative, entailing transcendence of the small self that chains us to petty, fear-based routine. Such commitment gives way to a phoenix-like transition, the willingness to stand in the fire of transformation and be delivered from the sphere of the small self to live for something greater.

Continually ask, "What would the best me do?" And choose the wholesome alternatives unconditionally. Choosing wholeness brings your true self into being without giving up who you are; it acknowledges our interconnectedness—alleviating aloneness and eliminating fear.

Realizing our greatest selves requires us to *commit, challenge,* and *choose*.

Commit

- Commitments—conscious and unconscious—define our character.
- Successful commitments move you toward desire, rather than away from fear.
- Greatness flows from consciously dedicating your strengths to a communal purpose.
- Love is your greatest strength. Like the sun, it is an endless source of energy.
- Committing to something worth living for makes you feel alive.

Challenge

- Extend unconditional love, beginning with yourself.
- Let go of the small self—less *I, me, my,* and more *you, we,* and *us.*
- Love others just as they are, seeing the potential in them.
- Periodically interrogate your beliefs and perspective.
- Liberate yourself from self-defeating stories that otherwise bind you to a small life.

Choose

- Choice, the exercise of will, is central to living into your greatness.
- Each moment offers a choice. Honor the moment by making the *right* choice.
- The voice of wisdom knows the right choices—the ones that bring more love into the world.

Choose Love

- Your purpose in living is to express love.
- You realize the fullest expression of love through wholeness.
- Wholeness emerges through the tens, perhaps hundreds, of healthy choices you make each day.
- Standing for love, you become whole and fulfill your potential.
- Love is the beginning of the end for everything you think is separate.
- Love unites what is (who you are) with what is possible (your greatest self).

PART 3: PRACTICE

I believe that we learn by practice. . . . Practice means to perform, over and over again in the face of all obstacles, some act of vision, of faith, of desire. Practice is a means of inviting the perfection desired. —Martha Graham

In theory there is no difference between theory and practice. In practice, there is. —Yogi Berra

Unless you have a few scars, you haven't truly lived. Tell me of your successes, and I may feel envy or awe; tell me of your mistakes and the lessons you have learned, and I will believe you are real. Those with the courage to speak of their journey from fear to love speak for all of us. Even with the greatest intentions, we all struggle, and sometimes we fail.

Maybe we hesitated to speak up when our support was needed. Or perhaps we did speak but drowned out a voice that needed to be heard. We sometimes fail to live in accordance with the resolutions we vow to uphold. Worse, we sometimes deliberately make unhealthy choices that undermine our greatness. Too often, we know exactly what the best me should do and still default on our commitments. But one of the beautiful things about the human spirit is that when we stumble and fall, we so often get up and try again.

The purpose of practice is to translate concepts into action. Through cultivating our voice of wisdom, we become better at making our thoughts, words, and deeds consistent with our guiding principles, and we learn to be proactive rather than reactive. Practice gives us power to create the state of being we desire through repeated thoughts, visualization, and feelings. We can learn to confront our challenges with confidence and conviction, tapping into our power and clearing the way for greatness.

Practice forms new habits over time. Metaphorically, practice wears a new path beside the existing track of reaction and futility. Just as some days you walk down a familiar street and think, *what a dreary neighborhood* or *the people in that house seem unfriendly*, on others, you might discover that not only is the neighborhood attractive in sunlight, but the old man you thought was unfriendly is smiling and waving from his porch.

Awareness of an alternative, more meaningful path creates the potential for a sustained transformation. Where once you felt only fear, you now envision ways to express love; where once you used your skills only for your own benefit, you willingly redeploy those skills to serve others as well. Once you commit to it, your practice begins to deepen and expand, both during the periods while you are consciously focused on it and in the interstitial time between. Like the spirit of a loved one far away, your practice becomes a constant presence hovering on the verge of awareness, integrated into your day, part of everything you do and the expression of who you are.

Lean forward

Lean forward to the next crazy venture beneath the skies. —Jack Kerouac

Although it seems perfectly natural, walking is an awkward, seemingly unnatural activity. Observed in slow motion, it looks more like controlled falling than deliberate locomotion. Standing perfectly balanced on two feet, we lean forward until we are about to fall. But just before crashing to the ground, we pitch a foot forward in time to catch our fall, then again as our other foot pivots past the first. Gravity takes care of the rest.

We are oblivious to the precariousness of walking until confronted with an unfamiliar environment, a flight of stairs with no handrail or the pitching deck of a ship at sea; under these unpredictable conditions, even the most coordinated among us must measure our steps—a momentary glimpse back to the time before we knew how.

Witnessing a child learning to walk is a marvelous thing. First they rock, then crawl, then pull themselves up—and often gawk slack-jawed at a world seen from a standing position for the first time. They wobble and reach out tentatively with an open hand and take a step. And then they fall down, a lot. They do this over and over, sometimes with a little thud and sometimes a spectacular crash, but they keep trying without understanding the mechanics of a body in motion, the words of spontaneous encouragement from the people around them, or the connection between intentions and success. They just practice. And slowly, over weeks or months, they begin to walk as if they were born on two feet.

The Power of 10 is a practice of leaning into our intentions until the gravitational force of wholeness pulls us into our next step. Like a child's first steps, any new practice feels awkward at first. For a time the practice feels mechanical and disorienting. Learning to integrate all perspectives and discern the truth requires us to lean forward and examine reality through inquiry by asking, *what do my body, heart, and mind agree to be true in each of the domains of my life?*

Once you arrive at an initial response to the inquiry, formulate your guiding principles, and begin to live into them, they pull you forward as if you are being drawn by gravity toward realizing your latent potential. By leaning in and taking a few tentative steps, you develop a self-sustaining way of life that becomes instinctual and effortless. And with each step, the practice increasingly becomes a natural part of your being.

Lose your balance

Courage doesn't always roar. Sometimes courage is the quiet voice at the end of the day saying, "I will try again tomorrow."
—Mary Anne Radmacher

To learn to walk, you must be willing to lose your balance, to stumble, and even to fall. Falling is natural. In fact, you're only really leaning forward when you feel as though you are about to fall. Otherwise, you are merely avoiding risk, either by setting low goals or by being too fearful to lean in.

The challenge is not to avoid stumbling or falling but in learning how to recover. Just like a toddler learns to walk, you get up, lean forward again, and take another step. Adults can reflect on the choices that preceded an event and acknowledge their mistakes:

- "That was thoughtless."
- "That was unhealthy."
- "That wasn't the best me."

Then let it go. The next moment presents the opportunity to start again, with the potential to make wholesome choices in alignment with your better self.

To keep from falling, you need only practice measuring your thoughts, words, and actions against your intentions. Your voice of wisdom serves as the steadying force to guide each step. It coaches or challenges you when change comes too slowly or encourages you in difficult moments. It is your companion wherever you go. During the workday, standing in line at the store on the way home from work, eating Sunday dinner with family—through practice you will build the muscle memory to be able to lean in even during periods of great difficulty. You will know you're on the right path, even when you stumble, even when you fall.

With regular practice, you can learn to judge less, understanding that failure is only temporary and a means to a greater end. Being harshly critical of yourself or others only wastes energy, leaving less available to focus on your goals.

Change is inevitable; how you respond to it is your choice. Through the practice of making healthy choices, you can build the capacity to transform your life *before* you stumble or fall. With each healthy choice, you feel a deepening immunity to suffering. As you learn how to do this effectively, your confidence grows.

Face resistance

What is happiness? The feeling that power increases—that resistance is being overcome. —*Friedrich Nietzsche*

There will be days when you don't want to practice. While there are many ways to the top of the mountain, none are easy; all require a long-term commitment. The status quo is a seductive plateau; the continuing challenge of leaning into your best self can become exhausting for you and for those around you.

Resistance to any serious discipline is expected. For example, perhaps you committed to getting up at 6:00 a.m. to run three miles, six days a week. Some days, though, you just want to sleep in. Whenever an unexpected surge of insurrection against some aspect of your practice arises, by acknowledging the part that remains resistant, you may discover an alternative. Maybe it's time to review your entire practice and to change a ritual you're not really enjoying anymore. If you find yourself sleeping in every morning instead of going for a run, perhaps it's not running that matters but simply being outside. In consulting your voice of wisdom you learn what part of the whole is being neglected.

An essential part of this or any other practice consists in simply overcoming internal resistance—the weight your psychic muscles encounter in adapting over time to get stronger. There is no substitute for the patience to give yourself and the practice a fair try. Real change takes time and is sometimes imperceptible as it is happening. To persevere, rely on your voice of wisdom—it knows the way.

Create a community of intention

Remember, we all stumble, every one of us. That's why it is a comfort to go hand in hand. —Emily Kimbrough

Taking on any new practice is challenging; it is easy to feel disoriented and confused at the beginning. Therefore, it can be helpful to build a community of intention around us. While it is still possible to transform ourselves without the support of like-minded people, transformative, wholesome change is difficult in isolation. Even with the best intentions, we often need others' help to remind us of our commitments.

The particular mechanics of a given practice are less important than the motives of the community. The most effective groups are founded on the *intention* to bring out the best in each of its members. We know we have found a good group when we feel both challenged and comforted as a member. The best groups resonate with our happiness and commiserate with our suffering while providing examples of how to move farther down our common path. The sustenance, inspiration, and accountability can make it a *pleasure* to stay on a path long enough to effect fundamental change.

It's also natural to want to share our experiences with others when we are making big changes—an urge that can disrupt our customary way of living. We need only think of the friend who suddenly became passionate about karate, the latest miracle diet, or an inspirational retreat and then felt compelled to convince us that we should follow his example. When our friends do this, sometimes we're put off by what we perceive to be proselytizing; other times, we're intrigued.

However, whenever we feel a surge of enthusiasm for our practice, it helps to remember our reactions to friends' efforts to share their new passions. While it is not healthy to conceal your practice from your friends—even if that were possible—neither is it helpful to impose new ideas on them. It's also important not to be discouraged by their indifferent or negative responses. For the philosopher Lao Tzu, practice was in the doing: "always practicing, sometimes speaking."

In integrating our practice into our lives, we sometimes find there are people who don't want us to change or who react to change in unexpected ways. These people count on us to be who we used to be so they can be who *they* are. Sometimes they need us to fulfill roles they don't want to play—but depend on nonetheless. Perhaps they have grown accustomed to a particular aspect of the relationship and want to sustain something we no longer experience. While it is natural and sometimes liberating to organize our lives around certain relationships, we also need space to evolve.

Fletcher and James, who work together, illustrate this point. Fletcher has always believed in punctuality and was not above gently chiding others who arrived late to meetings. James, on the other hand, was more fluid in his schedule and often late to meetings. When he joined Fletcher's team, James found himself the object of Fletcher's scolding and resented it. Like most people, James wanted the trains to run on time, unless he was the one late to the station.

Then one day, Fletcher changed. Tired of being "the enforcer," he just stopped speaking up. Not surprisingly, shortly after he dropped the role of punctuality enforcer, meetings started to drift off schedule. Even James became frustrated by the increasing disorganization of team meetings; he had actually grown to appreciate meetings starting and ending on time. But with Fletcher refusing to hold people accountable, James realized he would have to change his own behavior. If James wanted meetings to be on time, he would have to lean in and confront others about their punctuality.

When we begin any practice that affects our relationships with others, we inevitably cause our friends and loved ones to confront changes in their own lives. Some, especially family members or old friends, may even try to dissuade us from trying to improve our lives. This is a painful aspect of individuation: personal growth can shred long-term loyalties or open deep rifts in relationships when others don't respect our choices or impede our progress. But if we remain quietly steadfast and true to our purpose, those who care eventually embrace who we are becoming, even if they do not entirely agree with or even understand the practice. Some may come to find our inner light appealing and ask questions that betray a genuine interest. These are the people who will benefit from our sharing. And in giving voice to the nature of our own intentions, we more deeply discern the direction of our path.

Practice always; practice everywhere

Life is one indivisible whole. —Gandhi

Many years ago a Japanese monk moved to San Francisco to open a meditation center. At the time, meditation was not widely practiced in the West. The suspicion with which most San Franciscans viewed the exotic techniques of meditation was only increased by the fact the monk wore colorful robes and shaved his head. Who would consider learning anything from such a strange man?

It was easier for the monk when he first studied meditation. He began his practice in a Japanese monastery surrounded by like-minded monks who put meditation at the center of their lives. But in a foreign city with radically different traditions, the challenge of sharing his message with others seemed insurmountable. At first, the only people who would listen were drifters, homeless people, or curiosity seekers. He taught them anyway. Each day, he shared lessons on meditation, compassion, and love.

But he struggled. At night he retreated to his room, wondering whether he could bear another day. But he persevered and, over time, assembled a community that comprised people dedicated to improving their minds and lives, individuals from all walks of life and all religions. The only thing most members had in common was an interest in meditation and mindfulness. Some years later, after many Americans had come to understand and practice meditation, the monk was asked to describe how he had dealt personally with those difficult early days. His response: "All day I would teach about loving-kindness, and then all night I would cry because I had none."

Each of us has a mind like a temple. Within its walls it is easy to envision being our best selves. But practice is not a solitary exercise; real practice occurs outside our temples. Our journey really begins only when we walk outside the walls and take our practice into "real life," where we have something at stake.

Any practice is tempered by the daily confrontation with life. Everyone you meet carries their own world about them, one populated with its own commitments, beliefs, and attitudes. Collisions are inevitable. In such circumstances, it is important to recognize that the words and actions of others are more often a reflection of their own relationship to fear and love.

As you practice living into your purpose, it becomes easier to understand. That understanding allows you to infuse more and more of your being with wholeness. Because feeling whole gives rise to happiness, unhappiness is a signal that some aspect of your life is out of alignment with the whole. This absence of wholeness (or progress toward wholeness) can point to having "forgot-ten" the practices that would bring relief. In those moments when everything seems overwhelming, remember your ten-fingered emergency kit. Stop, take a deep breath, and recall the tools of inquiry:

- Who am I?
- How do I impact others?
- How will I spend this day?
- What is happening in this moment?
- How do we become our greatest selves?

Inquiry helps illuminate *what is*, while advocacy helps us to realize *what is possible*:

- Stand Tall
- Be Kind
- Plan Ahead
- Let Go
- Choose Love

The inquiries and advocacies are the complementary halves that evoke our voice of wisdom. This voice of wisdom helps us to connect to the essence of our being. Through

choosing to live into our purpose, we reawaken the wholeness given to us at birth and the happiness that emanates
from being whole. Our fingers are the ever-present guide
we can rely on.

When we give ourselves over to something greater without
reservation, simple rituals can tap a well of strength and
clarity. Using our fingers and the inquiries and advocacies
we assign to them, we can perform such a ritual. If you have
assigned inquiry to your left hand and advocacy to your right,
your fingers are your mnemonics.

During periods of inquiry, touch each of the fingers of your
left hand with your left thumb. As you touch each finger,
remind yourself to bring wholeness to the question associated with that finger. During periods of advocacy, touch the
fingers of your right hand with your right thumb to remind
yourself of the opportunity to choose love in every thought,
word, or action. Through Love, you are granted the power
to change the world.

Now that we have counted to ten together, it is time to
begin again. But this time it is your turn to ask the questions, to begin an inquiry into your own life. Choose your
guiding principles, whether these or others. Then, pound a
stake into the ground that marks the direction of your path,
knowing that even as you do, you may need to adjust your
course periodically. The challenge for each of us is the same:
to transform our instinct to save only ourselves into serving
the world.

So let us begin again with our first question:

Who am I?

APPENDIX 1: OUR TOOLKIT

1. *Who Am I?*

2. *How Do I Impact Others?*

3. *How Will I Spend This Day?*

4. *What Is Happening in This Moment?*

5. *How Do We Become Our Greatest Selves?*

 6. *Stand Tall*

 7. *Be Kind*

 8. *Plan Ahead*

 9. *Let Go*

 10. *Choose Love*

APPENDIX 2: DESCRIPTIVE TERMS

While any attempt to describe direct experience in mere words is inherently incomplete, the following definitions point toward the intended meaning of specific terms used within this work.

1: numerical representation of everything; an allusion to the practice of advocacy.

0: numerical representation of nothing; an allusion to the practice of inquiry.

10: numerical representation of the poles of everything/advocacy and nothing/inquiry, which is inclusive of the field between; an allusion to the flow of energy resulting from the tension between two seemingly contradictory but related positions or forces.

All/All That Is: every distinct part or being without exception (including me, you, and others).

beauty, truth, and goodness: the divine expression of body, heart, and mind, respectively.

being: both in the present (continuous) and existing (atemporally).

body, heart, and mind: distinct and connected fields of our being; also, the physical medium through which we experience the world (body); our connection to each other (heart); and the faculty to perceive, reason, and choose (mind).

character: attributes that define a person's right state of being.

compassion: a deep awareness of and sympathy for the suffering of another coupled with the desire to provide relief; the natural quivering of the heart in the face of pain or suffering.

conflict: any misalignment (or disunion) that impedes progress; a misalignment in thoughts, words, or actions of an individual or between two or more individuals or groups. *see also*: friction.

delusion: the lack of awareness or acceptance of reality often characterized by obsession, confusion, or helplessness.

divine: the nature of god, whether expressed as god, in silence, through nature, or by other manifestations.

domain: a territory of your life such as the domains of self, others, the future, and the present.

field: the space around and between a radiating body within which it can exert force on another body. For example, a heart may exert force on one's mind or another's heart.

flow: a harmonic body, heart, mind achieving sustained progress in a chosen activity.

free / freedom: free from suffering; choice without coercion. *see also*: whole freedom.

friction: anything that impedes the *velocity* of progress, particularly thoughts, words, or actions.

godlike nature or divine nature: the unique essence of the divine within each being expressed through beauty, truth, or goodness.

good: see *right*.

good/bad: preference described in terms of moral judgment. ". . . there is nothing either good or bad, but thinking makes it so." Shakespeare, *Hamlet*.

great/greater: larger than one.

greatest self or best self: the moment-by-moment practice of making the *right choice* in every domain of your life.

greatness: being your greatest self over time.

greed: the unhealthy expression of want or desire; insatiable desire.

happiness: sustained wellbeing and vitality that includes love, compassion, joy, and equanimity or peace; a byproduct of wholeness.

harmonic: congruity of parts with one another and with the whole; the *harmonic mind* associated with a flow state.

hatred: a variety of unwholesome emotions extending beyond simple anger, representing unhealthy reactions to the insecurity, imperfection, and impermanence inherent in life.

healthy: a derivation of "whole"; see *right*.

integrity: character expressing wholeness.

intention: a deliberately chosen purpose or outcome that guides one's thoughts, words, or actions.

is/isness: the current true nature or circumstances of something.

joy: the experience of pleasure.

judgment: providing answers before the question is formed.

living into: the moment-by-moment practice of aligning the body, heart, and mind to a positive intention or purpose until the resulting thoughts, words, and actions become a way of being.

Love (as distinct from love): the product of all wisdom; the sublime expression of the divine that unifies All as One; a power that has no opposite and is so great that our conscious mind cannot fully imagine it.

moments of being: an unbounded lightness/contentment of being associated with a place and time where we experience life in clear, vivid detail coupled with a deep sense of oneness with the object of our awareness; the eye of the harmonic flow.

one: a person, being, or organization.

One or Oneness: every distinct part without division, transcending and including All. (Sometimes referred to as the "Big I.")

positive: see *right*.

power: the will to achieve self-transcendence (wholeness) in the presence of resistance; a potentiality that exists or is actualized in a being's encounter with its internal and external environment.

preference: one's unique disposition toward a certain condition, character, or effect.

right: the positive or loving expression of a given thought, word, or action.

spirituality: the search for or direct experience of the divine; reunion with the divine.

suffering: greed, hatred, or delusion individually or in combination; an individual's basic experience of any unpleasant sensation, feeling, or emotion associated with harm or threat of harm.

thoughts, words, and actions: the respective expressions of the mind, heart, and body; collectively, your way of being.

true/truth: a fact verified through complete agreement of the body, heart, and mind. See also: *whole truth*.

true self/true you: a person's distinct essence (inclusive of preferences, experience, and perspective) of being as expressed through their thoughts, words, and actions. True self becomes the greatest self through right choices.

unhealthy: based in fear; alienation of wholeness.

whole: a fully realized individual or organism free of suffering; a fully integrated being realized through choosing to be your greatest self in each of the domains of your life.

whole freedom: unrestricted by any state of being, including life or death.

whole intelligence (WQ): the intelligences of our body (BQ) and heart (HQ) in conjunction with our mind (IQ).

whole self: the practice of being your *greatest self* in *all* the domains of your life; sometimes referred to as "unique self."

whole truth: universal agreement of a truth; a truth held by All without dissent.

wholeness/wholesomeness: state of being whole derived from the practice of being your *greatest self* in *all* the domains of your life over time.

Wisdom: the product of all knowledge and experience, without preference for either. See also *Love*.

APPENDIX 3: LIST OF COMMON VALUES

Health	Professionalism	Teamwork
Challenge	Effectiveness	Respect
Contribution	Adaptability	Adventure
Clarity	Empathy	Wisdom
Tradition	Harmony	Morality
Learning	Art	Innovation
Service	Consistency	Humility
Fairness	Friendship	Duty
Honesty	Freedom	Congruency
Reflectiveness	Growth	Intelligence
Leadership	Happiness	Flexibility
Journey	Simplicity	Patriotism
Non-judgment	Hope	Equality
Commitment	Service	Willingness to Change
Winning	Humor	Accountability
Community	Independence	Excellence
Supportiveness	Innovation	Empathy
Agility	Responsibility	Reputation
Fitness	Love	Balance
Reliability	Affection	Authenticity

Achievement	Loyalty	Wealth
Fun	Open-mindedness	Connection
Autonomy	Patience	Dependability
Beauty	Creativity	Understanding
Communication	Prosperity	Vitality
Strength	Risk-taking	Success
Courage	Quality	Music
Encouragement	Recognition	Power
Relationship	Trust	Productivity

ACKNOWLEDGMENTS

Principal Editor: Yolande McLean

Book Cover Design: Chin-Yee Lai

Typeface: Parisine and Tisa Pro

ENDNOTES

1 "Love is the foundation, not the negation, of power." — Paul Tillich, *Love, Power, and Justice: Ontological Analysis and Ethical Applications*

2 Worth noting is that our bodies, hearts, and minds serve respectively as the arbiters of ethos, pathos, and logos, the Aristotelian attributes of persuasion.

3 "I am a little pencil in God's hands. He does the thinking. He does the writing. He does everything and sometimes it is really hard because it is a broken pencil and He has to sharpen it a little more." —Mother Teresa, *The Joy of Loving: A Guide to Daily Living*

4 The binary symbol for 1+1 is 10.

5 "Photography is not like painting. . . . There is a creative fraction of a second when you are taking a picture. Your eye must see a composition or an expression that life itself offers you, and you must know with intuition when to click the camera. That is the moment the photographer is creative. Oop! The Moment! Once you miss it, it is gone forever."—Henri Cartier-Bresson

6 Maybe someday science or philosophy will answer the eternal questions of how life began, the nature of time, or what consciousness is, but we may never understand why we lose friends to disease, why we love so deeply, or how to communicate the experience of the sublime through words alone.

7 The Oak and the Willow: A conceited Willow had once the vanity to challenge his mighty neighbor the Oak to a trial of strength. It was to be determined by the next storm, and Aeolus was addressed by both parties, to exert his most powerful efforts. This was no sooner asked than granted; and a violent hurricane arose. The pliant Willow, bending from the blast, or shrinking under it, evaded all its force; while the generous Oak, disdaining to give way, opposed its fury, and was torn up by the roots. Immediately the Willow began to exult, and to claim the victory; when thus the fallen Oak interrupted his exultation: "Callest thou this a trial of strength? Poor wretch! Not to thy strength, but weakness; not to thy boldly facing danger, but meanly skulking from it, thou owest thy present safety. I am an oak, though fallen; though still a willow, though unhurt; but who, except so mean a wretch as thyself, would prefer an ignominious life, preserved by craft or cowardice, to the glory of meeting death in a honourable cause?"—Bewick's Selected Fables of Aesop and Others

8 "We Are What We Choose," Remarks by Jeff Bezos, as delivered to the Class of 2010 Baccalaureate on May 30, 2010: http://www.princeton.edu/main/news/archive/S27/52/51O99/

9 "Because we don't know when we will die, we get to think of life as an inexhaustible well. Yet everything happens a certain number of times, and a very small number, really. How many more times will you remember a certain afternoon of your childhood, some afternoon that's so deeply a part of your being that you can't even conceive

of your life without it? Perhaps four or five times more. Perhaps not even. How many more times will you watch the full moon rise? Perhaps twenty. And yet it all seems limitless." —Paul Bowles, *The Sheltering Sky*

10 After Congress approved the wording of the Declaration of Independence on July 4, about two hundred copies were printed. John Hancock, then President of the Continental Congress, sent a copy to General George Washington, instructing him to make it public. Before long, the Declaration was read to audiences and reprinted in newspapers across the thirteen colonies. The battle cry of independence struck a chord. Hearing it, crowds were moved to tear down and destroy signs and statues representing royal authority. In New York City, an equestrian statue of King George was pulled down and used to make musket balls. What the British labeled as "a few conspirators" seeking independence grew into a popular revolution.

11 Similarly, the Universal Declaration of Human Rights was explicitly adopted by the United Nations (by a vote 48 to 0) in 1948 following World War II as a declaration rather than a treaty. . . . This was done to influence the people of all nations as the Declaration of Independence had within the United States. . . . The Universal Declaration of Human Rights, created for the purpose of defining the meaning of the words "fundamental freedoms" and "human rights" that appear in the United Nations Charter, has served as the foundation for a growing number of international laws and treaties and has been adopted within or has influenced almost every national constitution created

since. . . . The scale of its impact is evidenced by the fact that the Universal Declaration of Human Rights is now the most translated document in history, having been translated and disseminated into more than three hundred languages and dialects across the world.

12 "The Good Samaritan Experiment" cited in Darley & Batson (1973).

13 Luke: 25-29.

14 See also autopoiesis.

15 Here is my secret. It is very simple: it is only with the heart that one can see rightly; what is essential is invisible to the eye.

16 You can almost hear the exchange:
Heart: I want to speak up more. I want to sing. I want to dance.
Head: Don't.
Heart: But why? I want to.
Head: Because you'll sound silly or weak, you'll lose control or you'll get hurt.
Heart: I don't want to get hurt, but I don't want to live like this either. Why can't I show how I really feel?
Head: You tried it before and you got hurt.
Heart: Not always.
Head: Have you forgotten the time you were broken? The time you were crushed? It will only happen again.
Heart: Yes... but...
Head: Stop it! I know what you will say: 'I survived' or 'It will be different this time.' It won't.
Heart: But I feel dishonest holding back. Especially with those I feel close to.

Head: Don't you remember? The closer the relationship, the more they can hurt you.

Heart: Hurt! I don't want to get hurt.

Head: Now you're getting it...Open up even a little and you will give them a thousand ways to hurt you.

Heart: It makes sense when you explain it that way.

Head: I am only trying to protect you.

17 The breakdown was (a) low hurry: 63 percent; (b) medium hurry: 45 percent; and (c) high hurry: 10 percent. The type of talk they were giving also had an effect on whether they offered help: Of those asked to talk about careers for seminarians, just 29 percent offered help, while of those asked to talk about the parable of the Good Samaritan, fully 53 percent gave assistance.

18 1 Corinthians 13:7-8.

19 In trying to define the word, the ancient Greeks divided the word "love" into no less than four categories: *éros*, the raw, naked, and powerful desire of sensual love that ignites the body; *storgē* and *philía*, the virtuous and loyal love of family and friends that warms the heart; and *agápe*, the unconditional, self-emptying love that lives in communion with the divine.

20 The complete quote: "Love until it hurts, love to infinity, love until there is no me left anywhere, only this radiant living Thou who bestows all glory, all goods, all knowledge, all grace, and forgives me deeply for my own manifestation, which inherently brings suffering to others, but which the loving God of the thou-ness of this moment can and does release, forgive, heal and make whole, but only if I can surrender in the core of my being,

surrender the self-contradiction through love and devotion and care and consciousness, surrender to the great
Thou as God or goddess, but here and now, radiant and
always, something-that-is-always-greater-than-me which
discloses the depths of this moment that are beyond the
I and the me and mine, beyond the self altogether, and
given to me by the Thou-ness of this moment, but only if
I can deeply and radically surrender in love and devotion
to the Great-Thou dimension of this now." —Ken Wilber,
Integral Spirituality

21 Unconditional commitments we might make to the
healthy expression of our intentions:

- It is healthy to use judgment; it is unhealthy to judge.
- It is healthy to share happiness; it is unhealthy to expect
  others to make us happy.
- It is healthy to love; it is unhealthy to use "love" to
  manipulate.
- It is healthy to want to succeed; it is unhealthy to crave
  recognition.
- It is healthy to compete; it is unhealthy to obsess about
  winning.

CPSIA information can be obtained at www.ICGtesting.com
Printed in the USA
LVOW08*0449060815

448763LV00003B/4/P